# HUNGER STRIKE

"Should be required reading for all anorectics ... but will also speak to all women."

*Booklist*

"Ms. Orbach extends feminist analysis systematically, convincingly and movingly to portray the anorectic struggle as a 'metaphor of our age.' It would be a shame to relegate HUNGER STRIKE to the 'women's' shelves."

*The New York Times Book Review*

"Susie Orbach is an undisputed expert on the subject of women and food."

*Birmingham Alabama News*

"Well-argued ... What is most interesting about HUNGER STRIKE is Orbach's philosophy for treating anorectics."

*Psychology Today*

# HUNGER STRIKE

## THE ANORECTIC'S STRUGGLE AS A METAPHOR FOR OUR AGE

# Susie Orbach

 **AVON**
PUBLISHERS OF BARD, CAMELOT, DISCUS AND FLARE BOOKS

AVON BOOKS
A division of
The Hearst Corporation
105 Madison Avenue
New York, New York 10016

First Avon Books Printing: March 1988

AVON TRADEMARK REG. U.S. PAT. OFF. AND IN OTHER COUNTRIES, MARCA
REGISTRADA, HECHO EN U.S.A.

Printed in the U.S.A.

K-R  10  9  8  7  6  5  4  3  2  1

To Audrey, Laura, Lisa and Jean
with respect and love

As we enter the 1980s, anorexia nervosa has become a symbol and leitmotif of the cultural forces in our society. The will to master and control one's selfhood and achieve absolute separateness and autonomy has become, for many Americans, the emblem of a safe existence. We find now a character style, exaggerated in the characterological structure of the anorectic, accentuating control and mastery with the central theme of realization of an ideal self, ideal body.

John Sours,
*Starving to Death in a Sea of Objects*

# Contents

# Foreword

This has been a painful book to write as the subject is indeed an anguishing one. In trying to represent the inner and outer world of the anorectic I have wished both to discuss anorexia *per se* and to relate its occurrence to wider social issues. I very much hope that in using the subject of anorexia nervosa as cultural comment, I have not in any way diminished the deeply personal concerns of individual anorectic women.

The making of this book has, as I said, been painful, but it has also been inspiring. In trying to come to grips with anorexia I have encountered a formidable strength and determination in individual women which has allowed me to understand how much of the anorexia is both an honorable protest and profoundly worthy cause. In working with the women who have let me enter their inner lives, I have been deeply moved and grateful for the opportunity to participate in their most intimate of struggles.

I would like to thank Frances Coady, Linda Healey and Caradoc King for the competence they have shown in their professional capacities towards this project.

*Susie Orbach*
*January 1985*

# Introduction

The rise in the incidence of anorexia has been accompanied by the spawning of numerous fictions about what it is, whom it affects and how to treat the sufferer. Like the meaning of the symptom itself, anorexia has been barely visible. It is seen as a new and frightening disorder. Until very recently training institutes, medical and graduate schools for psychiatrists, psychologists and social workers did not include study of it in their curricula. With the advent of interest a number of prejudices have grown up about anorexia. For example: it is morbid; it is untreatable; it creates resistant patients; it is a disorder of the pre-pubescent girl; it affects girls from upper-middle-class families; it shows up in high achievers and it is a flight from full genital sexuality. Treating anorexia has become a growth industry. Eating disorders in general are the hot topic in psychology, and the number of journal articles and dissertations on the subject is soaring. Similarly, clinics and training programs in eating disorders are proliferating to serve the medical and mental health practitioners confronting the growing number of cases of anorexia.

A feature of this new interest has been the attempt to provide a useful classification and nosology.[1] This stems in part from the obviously problematic use of the word anorexia—which literally means loss of appetite—to describe a syndrome that is about the denial and overriding of hunger and appetite. Other difficulties arise from the wish to describe succinctly observed differences in the cases practitioners meet, presumably with the aim of fitting a treatment model to a particular pattern. In this book I use anorexia in its broadest possible sense to describe those women who are invested in not eating and have become scared of food and what it can do to them. Although it contains features of both compulsive eating and bulimia, as an anorectic woman will from time to time binge and throw up, the most obvious thing about anorexia is the persistence of the sufferer's food refusal. She desperately wants to be thin and she transforms her body dramatically to this end. In fact she becomes so small that she loses the minimum amount of body weight at which she will menstruate. What she does eat is so minimal, so calculated and controlled in its intake, that her body becomes literally starved of nutrients. She develops a cluster of physical symptoms. Her extremities become sensitive to cold, she can hardly sleep and becomes an early riser. A soft, downy hair grows all over her body to keep her warm. In other words, the anorectic is involved in a serious and successful transformation of her body. The compulsive eater fantasizes that everything in her life would be better if she were thin, indeed she wishes she could catch a month's worth of anorexia. But the contentment the anorectic so desired to reach through thinness eludes her, and a transformation then occurs in the thrust and the meaning of the symptom. The anorectic becomes utterly absorbed in maintaining the various schemes she has devised to rid herself of the little food she consumes.

While the anorectic comes to fear taking in food for herself, she feels the need to be near it. She thinks about it constantly, is involved in preparing food for others, especially desserts, and shows concern for the food needs of those close to her. In this way her own desire and need for food is partly met through the process of projective identification. The little food she does allow herself to eat is taken in private. When forced to eat in the company of others, a woman suffering from anorexia moves the food around her plate, burying it in napkins or under salad leaves. She is terrified of taking it in and losing the control she has struggled to create.

On the one hand, anorexia is about being thin—very, very thin. It is an expression of a woman's confusion about how much space she may take up in the world. On the other hand, her food denial is driven by the need to control her body which is, for her, a symbol of emotional needs. If she can get control over her body, then perhaps she can similarly control her emotional neediness. Submitting her body to rigorous discipline is part of her attempt to deny an emotional life. The anorectic cannot tolerate feelings. She experiences her emotional life as an attack on herself, and she attempts to control it so that she will not be devoured by her emotions. She tries to gain control over her body and her mind by creating an altogether new person out of herself. In other words, she negates who she is—needy, hungry, angry, yearning—and through the adoption of strenuous diet and exercise rituals turns herself into someone she finds more acceptable. In turn her submission to the rituals creates a boundary between herself and her needs. She gathers strength from the knowledge that she can ignore her needs and appetites.

## BULIMIA

Although this book is concerned chiefly with anorexia, it is well noted that many anorectic women go through bulimic episodes. Bulimia as a well-defined syndrome is an even more recently observed condition. One way in which it has been noted is in the growing phenomenon of what I would classify as episodic bulimia, which is currently spreading through college campuses in much the same way that marijuana did some fifteen to eighteen years ago.

Bulimia is frequently a social activity in which women students get together, gorge themselves and then evacuate. While in its activity it reproduces the painful bulimia that involuntarily grips many women, this is not an entrenched or addicting habit for many of those who indulge only occasionally. The parallel with marijuana is apt, for many social bulimics who engage in the activity as a special form of bonding are quite capable of giving it up. Bulimia is not the soft symptom on the way to anorexia, just as marijuana is not the soft drug on the way to heroin. For some women it *is* a prelude to anorexia and for other women it is a serious problem in itself, like the continual use of marijuana. For those women who experience themselves as in a slavish relation to binging and evacuating, the following description might ring true and offer some ideas about ways of thinking about the activity. As I have indicated, for some women anorexia is accompanied by bulimic features on a daily basis. Bulimia, like its sister syndromes of compulsive eating and anorexia, is undoubtedly an alternative response by women to the conditions of their upbringing and the wider social world as discussed in this book. For this reason, aspects of the social analysis may well apply equally to bulimic women.[2]

Unlike the anorectic woman, the bulimic woman will eat in public—although she may excuse herself after a meal to throw up—and she will not show the same kind of intense interest in talk of food or recipes. On the outside she may look just as she is supposed to, i.e. slim but not emaciated. In other words there is not the same broadcast announcement to the world that something is wrong. The bulimic's survival mechanism is the fact that she gorges and gorges and has a way of seemingly not paying for what she sees as her greed. She gets rid of the food, usually by bringing it up, sometimes by massive intakes of laxatives. No one necessarily knows that she is in trouble with food. She looks all right—even if she herself doubts it—and she seems to eat very reasonably. If she is relatively thin, she is unable to draw much comfort from having achieved such a body size, for she feels herself to be a fraudulent thin. In her own mind she is getting away with something. She is delicately perched on a binge–vomit seesaw that could betray her.

During the daytime fragments of emotional shrapnel pierce the bulimic woman's insides. She hurts but has few resources for living with or passing through her pain. Unconsciously she pushes the emotions aside until later. She performs her job competently, and her emotional exterior—just like her physical one—belies that she has a problem. She seems even-tempered, good-natured and able to take the knocks of everyday life easily. But she lives a split life, for inside she is all wrenched up. She cannot let things bounce off her, and is very sensitive and easily wounded. She tries to keep out the hurt she experiences by day, and by night she has an emotional and physical binge. Her binge is an intense experience. In it she may feel like a wild animal, foraging, searching, desperately looking for something to soothe and satisfy her. All the feelings that lay undigested by day, jump out at her as though the spring from Pandora's box has been released. But still the woman cannot embrace them or examine them. They terrify her so that she goes towards food in an attempt to quell and bury them.

The bulimic woman finds very little solace in the experience of eating. She will not feel better until she has filled and then emptied herself out. She needs to cleanse herself, to deny the need for soothing, to throw up and out of herself what she cannot digest. The process of not being able to keep what she wants inside her is reiterated. The bulimic behavior continually short-circuits the discovery of what is troubling her deep down. Bulimic episodes are almost like substitute dramas. This does not mean that they are not real, terrifying or humiliating, difficult or painful in themselves; but they are encapsulated experiences, ink blobs on a handwritten page. They mar an otherwise perfect-looking copy book. They are dark and messy expressions of an inner turmoil she cannot eradicate.

When the bulimic, or anorectic woman who is about to have a binge, begins, she may start off with a colorful marker such as tomato juice. After bringing up the food, she will wait to see the orange liquid to reassure herself that nothing has been absorbed. She becomes fantastically preoccupied with the ritual of binging and vomiting. It may take several hours, or the whole evening and night too. She can travel from deli to diner eating a meal at each, or she can shut herself up at home with several cakes, tubs of ice cream, cheese and crackers, and ingest, throw up, ingest, throw up. The binging becomes a totally absorbing activity, a way of spending time with herself and coping with her life.

Although the treatment of bulimia presents many interesting and complex issues for the therapist,[3] the treatment programs and new clinics designed mainly to address the rise in anorexia give us no cause to be sanguine about the results they generate. There is a discouragingly high failure rate in the treatment of anorexia. In spite of the variety of approaches from psychoanalysis to behavior modification, present treatment models share the common assumption that the anorectic is willful and stubborn in her refusal to eat. This refusal is so annoying to practitioners and so terrifying to family and friends that interventions focus almost entirely on attempting to make the woman give up the refusal. When the anorectic is unable to comply with the dietary plan offered, she may well be force-fed. In civilized hospitals throughout the United States and England, doctors are perfecting ever more elegant techniques to bypass women's mouths and push food into their stomachs. The general consensus is that the patient has recovered when the normal weight is reached and appropriate sex role functioning is achieved.

Such interventions reflect, at best, only superficial attempts to understand the problem, and the goals they are meant to achieve are inevitably short-lived. Further, such treatments are paradoxical. The woman cannot maintain the weight gain, and her original insecurity and lack of self-esteem are amplified. In the anorectic denial she could achieve some private form of success, a sense of achievement. Now she feels she is failing again.

Cognitive approaches, by far the most common, assume that if only the anorectic could be made to see what she is up to, she would be able to give up her troublesome and difficult behavior. However well-reasoned, such approaches cannot possibly penetrate to the level of the unconscious except as further judgments. For anorexia is not so much a conscious act of will (although it contains elements of that) as an unconscious solution to a set of inter- and intra-psychic problems that cannot be met another way. For the anorectic, the denial is a *strength*, it gives her a sense of accomplishment. Frequently it is the only aspect of her behavior that gives her a feeling of pride. Engaging in combat at the level of ideas thus misses her experience and obstructs the possibility of helping.

For the last decade and a half, colleagues at The Women's Therapy Centre in London and The Women's Therapy Center Institute in New York have been engaged in developing a perspective on eating problems which, by taking account of the social position of women, offers a new means of understanding and generating treatment models useful to those suffering from compulsive eating, bulimia or anorexia. I have detailed aspects of the work on compulsive eating in *Fat is a Feminist Issue* and *Fat is a Feminist Issue II*. In this book the social analysis in part 1 provides the background for the case studies and vignettes in part 2, and suggests a new treatment protocol for anorexia. It is my hope that what frequently appears as an intractable problem will become less forbidding as the meanings of the complex of psychological and physical responses are revealed. At the same time, I hope I will make comprehensible the discomforting fascination and repulsion that onlookers can experience when they view the anorectic's cadaverous body. Above all I hope that in speaking directly to the anorectic's experience, she will feel understood and empathetically presented on the page.

The anorectic women I am writing about do not conform to the stereotyped picture of the resistant adolescent, morbid, upper-middle-class young woman widely considered to be the prime sufferer. To be sure, I have met many adolescent young women in the course of my work but I have also had the privilege to work with a grandmother of sixty, a woman who had lived with anorexia over the course of many, many years, and with many women well into adulthood. In most cases the women were not dragged to therapy but came themselves, despite enormous hesitancy and fear. They have been from working-class backgrounds and middle-income groups. They have included those who are academically inclined and those who are prostitutes. While the features of the anorexia that develops (the defense structure) are similar in each case, and so a discussion of symptomatology would render these women one-dimensional, a most obvious thing about all the women

I have worked with is that the pattern of symptoms covers a rich variety of experience. The overwhelming commonality of experience is not at the level of activity, age or station in life, but is revealed in the shared conceptions of the kind of emotional life deemed permissible, ideas that arise from attempts to understand and deal with unmet emotional need, desire and authentic initiations. In each instance of anorexia one can observe the most brutal internal struggle directed at suppression of needs that originate from inside the woman. The evidence of a need is felt as threatening to a self-image which is based on effacement. If anorexia is always an attempt at negating need, the question is why these women's needs are so fraught and why privation is so highly valued. The answer, I will argue, lies in the particularly heightened sensitivity that these women have absorbed from an early age about the ways in which they are to live *as women*. The individual woman's problem—for which the anorexia has been the solution—is that despite a socialization process designed to suppress her needs, she has continued to feel her own needs and desires intensely. She has not successfully come to terms with negotiating those internal desires either by being able to meet them or by binding them up with ease. Her anorexia is the daily, even hourly, attempt to keep her needs in check, to keep herself and her desires under wraps. In dominating her existence, anorexia negates the force of other needs. In demanding a superhuman submission to denial it provides a self-contained and reliable way of being.

Whenever woman's spirit has been threatened, she has taken the control of her body as an avenue of self-expression. The anorectic refusal of food is only the latest in a series of woman's attempts at self-assertion which at some point have descended directly upon her body. If woman's body is the site of her protest, then equally the body is the ground on which the attempt for control is fought.

## NOTES

1. See Bruch, H., *Eating Disorders: Obesity, Anorexia Nervosa and the Person Within* (New York, 1973); Crisp, A.H., *Let Me Be* (London and New York, 1980); Sours, J.A., *Starving to Death in a Sea of Objects* (New York, 1980); Wellbourne, J. and Purgold, J., *The Eating Sickness* (Sussex, 1984).

2. I have not chosen, however, to address directly the problems of those women who would define themselves or be defined as bulimic because my clinical experience with exclusively bulimic women is limited.

3. In therapy we need to examine the tension between in and out, the rhythm of ingestion and expulsion. We need to address the question of why the woman feels so terribly threatened by food. We need to help her find out why she cannot keep something first perceived as good and comforting, inside her. We need to discover what it is that is so dreadful about her that she must throw up the food she first saw as soothing. We need to understand what it is about a potentially soothing experience that invariably contains its opposite. We need to know what it is about taking in good feelings that turns them poisonous so fast. We need to understand together why she must repudiate the solace.

# PART I

# 1 Anorexia: Metaphor for Our Time

Every morning hundreds and thousands of women wake up worrying about whether it is going to be a "good day" or a "bad day" in relation to food. They feel remorse for what they ate yesterday and hope that they will have more control today. They approach the day with dread or hope according to how in control of food they feel. That food routinely plagues women is an acknowledged and discussed aspect of everyday life. An obsessive involvement with food flows out of a cultural insistence that what they eat, how much they eat, and how they cook for others, is their especial domain. Food is the medium through which women are addressed; in turn, food has become the language of women's response.

The preoccupation with food is linked with a fetishizing of the female form. Women wish to acquire that elusive, eternally youthful body beautiful. A woman's body becomes the subject of scrutiny, the recipient of enormous amounts of attention, and the vehicle for the expression of a wide range of statements. Women find themselves obsessively engaged with both their food and their bodies. A woman's body is the beneficiary of hours of attention, worrying and fretting. But at the same time, the pain of being caught up in a never-ending battle to get one's body right (and the eating behaviors that follow from this) is somehow muted. Women are constantly engaged in trying to mediate the harrowing effects of culturally induced body insecurity. This preoccupation is both a hidden and a public state of affairs. Women accept—at some level—the importance of self-presentation, and so obsession with the body is a permitted form of self-expression and self-involvement for them. But this publicly sanctioned private activity hides the deeply anguished relationship that so many women come to have with their bodies. Women repress the knowledge of how damaging and hurtful this obsession is.

Anorexia nervosa is perhaps the most dramatic outcome of the culture's obsession with regulating body size. In the last ten years this psychological syndrome has risen to epidemic proportions.[1] The potential reader may well demur and ask, "What has all this to do with me? What could there be of possible wide interest in a cultural and clinical study of anorexia?" The same reader may well go further and admit to an active disinterest in, perhaps even a revulsion for, the subject. But although the anorectic response to our cultural conditions may strike one as extreme, perhaps off-putting and bizarre, the very extremeness of the response illuminates the experience of women today. Anorexia nervosa—self-starvation—is both a serious mental condition affecting thousands upon thousands of women, and a metaphor for our age. Like the psychological symptom of hysteria that Freud described so well in late nineteenth-century Vienna, anorexia nervosa is a dramatic expression of the internal compromise wrought by Western women in the 1980s in their attempt to negotiate their passions and desires in a time of extraordinary confusion. But whereas hysteria was an "imagined" physical response to emotional distress caused by the imprisoning feminine role of the Victorian period, what occurs in anorexia nervosa is the excruciating spectacle of women actually *transforming* their bodies in their attempts to deal with the contradictory requirements of their role in late twentieth-century America and England.

Such psychological symptoms are the understudies for the unspeakable. They express both the rebellion and the accommodation that women come to make in the context of a social role lived within circumscribed boundaries. The starvation amidst plenty, the denial set against desire, the striving for invisibility versus the wish to be seen—these key features of anorexia—are a metaphor for our age.

Psychological symptoms and the meanings sought in them by analysts and analysands render alive the unconscious world of the individual in her time. Decoded, these symptoms allow us to enter, in the most detailed way, women's everyday experience. As windows into generalizable experience they call attention to deeply painful but salient aspects of women's existence which are so often obscured.

The most commonly held view of anorexia is that it is the female's refusal to be an adult.[2] It is a disorder of puberty, an attempt to stay a girl, a denial of femininity. If we examine the implications of this perspective, we can see that it has two aims, both of which distinctly infantilize the woman. For, once seen as a child, the anorectic woman becomes much less of a threat—the meaning of her symptom is delegitimized. It becomes mere unacceptable behavior, to be dealt with summarily, and the sufferer's opinions become discountable because, like herself, they are immature.

Behind the notion that this is a disorder of puberty, lies another unquestioned assumption. Grown-up femininity is assumed to be unproblematic. The anorectic's refusal to accept her culturally defined role is seen to be *per se* pathological, not an extremely complicated response to a confusing social identity. Even the most forward-thinking of practitioners who proffer help to anorectics use this model as a basis for their work. Inevitably they are caught up in a dilemma as they find themselves engaged in a power struggle with a very persistent and tenacious person. They become enmeshed in a paradox, for on the one hand they describe the anorectic as weak and childish, and on the other hand they experience her as a crafty, strong and unyielding opponent. Trying to reconcile their view of her as childlike with her relentless pursuit of incomprehensible aims, they end up involved in what can only be described as a struggle for power over who is to control the individual woman's body. Force-feeding, enforced bed rests, forcing women to be taken by wheelchair to the toilet and supervised once there, may at first glance seem benevolent. The 70-lb. patient is weak and she requires the utmost care and attention.[3]

A more serious consideration of such treatment procedures, however, draws uncomfortable parallels with general cultural attitudes towards women's bodies. For these measures in reality reflect a kind of rape *par excellence* of the female body—an intrusion so brutal and invasive that in seeking an explanation I am forced to posit the existence of a need, albeit an unconscious one, to control women. Such measures, though startling, are simply a by-product of accepted cultural practices which run the gamut from the seemingly innocuous dictating of a female aesthetic, or the routine blaming of women for male sexual assaults, to practices more generally regarded as horrifying, such as foot-binding and clitorectomies.

Such a need to control the female body is not new. Indeed, contemporary medical attitudes towards anorexia have much in common with the attitudes of nineteenth-century physicians to the debilitating feminine occupation of hysteria. Hysteria was a condition assigned to women in the same way that eating problems today are considered endemic to women's existence. Although we are accustomed to thinking of hysteria as the disease of the bourgeois woman, it cut across class lines in both the United States and England. In the earlier part of the nineteenth century imprecise nosology meant that hysteria gathered into itself all manner of distress symptoms. Some of these by definition cancelled each other out, others meant that "hysteria" became a convenient catchall for any kind of physical or mental stress experienced by women. While working-class women with hysteria were considered shirkers, treating the middle-class woman became the (financial) backbone of the gentleman doctor's practice. Contemporary accounts reveal a striking similarity between the attitudes of the nineteenth-century doctors and those who treat anorectics today.[4] Indeed, even the actual language in which Weir Mitchell, the most famous and respected American woman's doctor of the 1880s, describes the "deceitfulness" of hysterics, is chillingly close to that used in describing the willful, intransigent anorectic.[5] But it is not simply the congruence of *attitudes* towards women's disorders that should concern us. More striking and more worrying are the parallels that can be seen in the *treatment* of the nineteenth-century hysteric and today's anorectic.

Weir Mitchell recommended a strict "rest cure" accompanied by "fattening up."[6] His prescriptive measures would not be out of place in a large number of hospital divisions dedicated to the treatment of anorexia today: a rich diet, attention from the doctor, and the acceptance of the wisdom of the doctor's interventions. The nineteenth-century feminine ideal of frailty and romance which found such marked expression in the literature and the illnesses of Victorian women, rests on a view of women as the inherently inferior and weaker sex. The fainting, pains and state

of immobility that the "hysteric" achieved in a number of
ingenious ways were responded to with the demand that
she accept her weakness and take to her bed.

While such treatments were hardly barbaric in the
nineteenth-century context they failed to address the deeper
causes of a woman's listless malaise. As the Women's
Movement was to demonstrate emphatically, the problem
of hysteria was not so much the result of overactivity as
the result of inactivity or a regimen of sequestered and
limited activity. As Freud would discover, the hysterical
stance covered a voice of protest. Hysteria was the exaggeration of idealized womanliness, but in its very caricature of femininity it contained an implicit indictment.

Current treatment programs in which anorectics are fat-
tened up at the rate of 5,000 calories a day and required to
endure total bed rest[7] are merely old wine in new bottles.
But it is old wine that was medically suspect when first
bottled and has proved to have even less beneficence when
recirculated.

If the scope of the problems, the way they are conceived, and the treatment attitudes that flow from such a
perspective are so similar, what is illuminated by situating
hysteria and anorexia in their separate social contexts?
Carol Smith-Rosenberg argues that in the midst of a situation of enormous social and structural upheaval and change
in the nineteenth century, opportunities for women remained essentially domestic, and within that sphere, the
roles were few and rigid. From this perspective hysteria
can be seen as an alternative role option for particular
women incapable of accepting their life situation. Hysteria
thus serves as a valuable indicator both of domestic stress
and of the tactics through which some individuals sought
to resolve them.[8]

Eventually, a public response on the part of women to
this state of affairs emerged. It was evidenced by the

appearance of a boisterous and energetic suffragette movement. This political movement was not marked by the
niceties of nineteenth-century convention surrounding wom-
en's activities. Indeed, as their cause was refused so the
tactics they employed to achieve their ends extended to
law breaking which in turn led to imprisonment. Once
imprisoned, the suffragettes refused the silence of their
new confines and forced a public awareness of their presence and hence their aims. They went on hunger strike and
in so doing entered into a struggle with representatives of
the state—the prison governors and Home Office officials—
about the consequences of the government's attempt to
control their minds. A new battle ensued in which control
of food became the expression of deeper political power.
Women contested the legitimacy of the government by
their refusal to eat. The government's response to this
protest in the form of force-feeding is yet another example
of the notion that control of the female body is not something that resides with its owner, the individual woman,
but is an area to be contested.

By contrast, and of course due in no small measure to
the public activities of the suffragettes, women today are
presented with an apparently bewildering number of social
role options. One only has to choose what one wishes and
the world is open. Where narrow role-definition previously
imprisoned women, now variety, opportunity and unlimited possibilities exist. Or rather, so goes the myth. At the
heart of the new possibilities for women, anorexia illuminates the difficulties of entry into a masculinist world. The
anorectic woman encompasses in her symptom a way of
being entirely at odds with the phlegmatic response of her
nineteenth-century hysterical sister. Not for her the fainting,
falling or flailing fits; her protest is marked by the achievement of a serious and successful transformation of her
body, that same body that her great-great-grandmother used

as a weapon in her own time. Rather than collapsing because of "feminine frailty," the anorectic woman today, in losing the defining curves of femininity and in ceasing to menstruate, does away with the explicit marker of her reproductive capacities. In essence she defeminizes her body. Interestingly, where possibilities are so apparently multiple and fluid, a woman's symptomatic response is narrow, rigid and controlled. Where nineteenth-century possibilities for women were few and narrowly defined, the woman's expression and unconscious protest through her symptom was in turn unbounded.

Participation in the modern world involves the pursuit of success for its own sake and as defined by our culture rather than an evaluation of the basis of this world. In spite of the rhetoric of women's equality, feminine values have not been assimilated outside the domestic sphere. Women entering the world beyond the home do so as guests and not as principals; the necessary shifts, adjustments and negotiations are contingent on women making them. Women are required to accommodate themselves to the public sphere much as they accommodate others in private. Even if they are no longer relegated to the role of mere midwives to the activities of others, they must nevertheless ensure that their presence is quasi-unobtrusive. They must conform to prevailing masculinist values and accept entry on that basis.

The late twentieth century has failed to bring about a substantially new role relationship between men and women. To be sure, women's work is now more visible and discrimination on job training and job entry is couched in apologetic terms. Reformist struggles taken up by the second wave of feminism have made for dramatic improvements and changes in the lives of many, many women. However, American women still live in a society in which the Equal Rights Amendment remains unratified, while the legal equality granted to English women has been found to be inadequately legislated and enforced. These manifestations of women's continued inequality are reflected in both subtle and crude ways in the family, education, the health system and the world of work. Equality has little chance of being consolidated if society is not, even in principle, committed to it. Even with legal protection, if equality is to enter the hearts, experience and day-to-day reality of contemporary men and women, it requires a concerted struggle at every level—a questioning of our most basic assumptions and society's commitment to change. No such move has been initiated at a state level. No commitment to the examination and change of male and female roles has been undertaken. In this context the woman of today faces contradictory pulls. She is culturally and psychologically prepared for a life in which she should continue to service the needs of others, while at the same time she is teased with the possibility of living a life for herself. These themes enter directly into current child-rearing practices where children observe and experience upbringing in a predominantly female ambience while receiving the "new" message that the world outside of the home is the domain of all. Femininity is inextricably linked with the home and with mothering. The new femininity outside the home depends upon the assuming of masculine values or the extension of the feminine role into the work force in the form of service work.

Today women from every generation experience themselves being pushed and pulled in opposing directions. While individual women can find a way to balance new possibilities and pressures, all women live with a tension about their place in the world. This tension is not immediately obvious from women's psychological symptoms, and it may not be consciously articulated. However, as we investigate the meaning of anorexia we are presented with an extremely graphic picture of the internal experience of contemporary femininity. Anorexia symbolizes the restraint on women's desires. In the most tortuous denial of need and dependency and the most persistent and insistent expression of independence, women with anorexia live out the contrariness of contemporary cultural dictates.

The Women's Liberation Movement and recent feminist scholarship provide us with a context for looking at women's relationship with their psychological symptoms, and with food and their bodies.[9] Prefeminist analyses or approaches that ignore feminism suffer from an inability to comprehend why women are involved in such complicated, and in the case of anorexia, savage, struggles with food and body-image. In failing to comprehend the thrust behind anorexia, compulsive eating and bulimia, practitioners throw up their arms in despair or mechanically "treat" the sufferer as though she were at best an oddity, at worst an offending object. In trying to get her to eat and to become the "right size" they negate her protest. They unwittingly deny the meaning of her symptom and in so doing contribute to its perpetuation. They become part of the problem rather than part of the solution.

By recasting the terrain on which psychological inquiry is based, feminism allows us to hear with different ears the stories of women who suffer with anorexia. In taking as a starting point the fact that woman's social role creates her particular psychology, feminism illuminates how woman's psychology reflects both a preparation for her social role as well as her rebellion against it. Psychologies are gender-specific and each individual psyche comes to embody the ensemble of social relations. If we reflect upon the meaning of "food," "fat," "thin" and "femininity," we see that these words conjure up many layered pictures of social practices which involve and affect us all.

Women's relationship with "food," "fat," "thin" and

"femininity" is at once extremely complex and extremely simple. Two imperatives underlie it which in turn become highly elaborated. The first of these is that throughout history we know the female form as an object of pleasure for men. This aspect of femininity is insinuated into each woman's experience of self, and finds expression in each woman's relationship with her body. In their passage towards femininity, all girls experience the pressure to be attractive, to make their bodies conform to the designated ideal of the day, to be slender, tall, blonde, curvaceous, slim-hipped, round-bottomed, or pointed-breasted. The second imperative is the paradoxical relationship of woman with food and feeding. She must feed others but restrain her own desires for that very same food. An unquestioned aspect of women's experience today is each woman's knowledge that she will inevitably be dieting or manipulating her own intake of food in one way or another. The elaboration of these themes in this book is an attempt to provide an explanation for the increase of anorexia, and eating problems of all kinds, in women today.

The insights of feminism make possible a compassionate reading of the anorectic response. In deciphering this psychological symptom we can see that the anorectic woman has shaped for herself a particularly extreme, intense and rebellious relationship with the various struggles facing women. She has changed her body dramatically. She has become slimmer and smaller as today's aesthetic demands, but so emaciated that her body is an indictment of proposed feminine sexuality. She has agreed to take up only a little space in the world, but at the same time, her body evokes immense interest on the part of others and she becomes the object of their attention. Her invisibility screams out. We cannot avert our eyes from her. In controlling her food so very stringently she caricatures the messages beamed at all women. She is not the passive victim of the diet doctor, however, as *she* remains supremely in charge and *active* in relation to the suppression of her bodily needs. In denying her needs—as women are so often reminded to do—she excels as the "good girl" who refuses to make demands on others. At the same time she steadfastly attempts to meet those needs within herself. Her anorexia is at once an embodiment of stereotyped femininity and its very opposite.

## NOTES

1. Duddle, M., "An Increase of Anorexia Nervosa in a University Population," *British Journal of Psychiatry,* 123 (1973), 711–12; Crisp, A.H., Palmer, R.L. and Kalucy, R.S., (1976) "How Common is Anorexia Nervosa? A Prevalence Study," *British Journal of Psychiatry,* 128, (1976), 549–54.

2. See, for example, Crisp, A.H., *Let Me Be* (London and New York, 1980).

3. Van Buskirk, S.S., "A Two-phase Perspective on the Treatment of Anorexia Nervosa," *Psychological Bulletin,* 84 (1977), 529–38; Lucas, A.R., Duncan, J.W., and Piens, V., "The Treatment of Anorexia Nervosa," *American Journal of Psychiatry,* 133 (1976), 1034–8.

4. See, for example, Crisp, *op. cit.,* and Mitchell Weir, S., *Fat and Blood* (Philadelphia, 1881); Skey, F.C., *Hysteria* (New York, 1867).

5. Mitchell Weir, S., *Lectures on the Diseases of the Nervous System, Especially in Women* (New York, 1881), as cited by Carol Rosenberg-Smith, "The Hysterical Woman: Sex Roles in Nineteenth Century America," *Social Research,* 39, 652-78.

6. Mitchell Weir, *op. cit.*

7. Russell, G.F.M., "Anorexia Nervosa: its Identity as an Illness and its Treatment," in *Modern Trends in Psychological Medicine* ed. Price, J.H. (London, 1970).

8. Smith-Rosenberg, *op. cit.*

9. Orbach, S., *Fat is a Feminist Issue* (New York and London, 1978); Orbach, S., *Fat is a Feminist Issue II* (New York and London, 1982); Lawrence, M., *The Anorexic Experience* (London, 1984); Ehrenreich, B., and English, D., *For Her Own Good* (New York, 1978); Chernin, K., *Womansize* (London, 1983).

# 2 Situating Anorexia

Anorexia nervosa, first reported by Richard Morton in 1694,[1] has shown a dramatic rise during the past twenty years, and more especially in the last decade.[2] It is no longer a physician's curiosity. Nearly every branch of medicine and psychiatry, including dentistry, gastro-enterology, and gynecology, meets with anorectics in the course of regular practice, and many areas of medicine now contribute to the growing body of literature being assembled about the etiology, course and treatment of anorexia nervosa. This account of anorexia, together with the explanation offered for its recent dramatic rise, builds on work in women's psychological and social development within two areas of scholarship: theoretical and clinical work on the construction of a feminine psychology,[3] and theoretical and clinical work on eating problems in general.[4]

The rise in the incidence of anorexia nervosa provides us with an unusually visible example of the way in which psychic structure and symptom formation are determined by three factors: the social climate of a period; particular models of parenting; and the attempt of each generation to find its place in the world. This section of the book examines how these influences interact and how the tensions within each one are expressed. In trying to explain the features of this distress symptom, I will draw on sociological evidence important in explaining its locus.

The last twenty-five years in Europe and the last thirty in the United States have witnessed the emergence of what is commonly called the consumer society. The social rationale for mid- and late twentieth-century capitalism is that in contrast with all other systems, it delivers the goods that people want. The economy is organized around a capricious marketplace eager for more and more consumer goods (at first durables, increasingly luxury toys). Capitalism is proclaimed as the most responsive of economic systems and the most technologically advanced. Since the Second World War, the mass of people have had access to a wider and wider range of goods such as cars and television, and have enjoyed a higher level of prosperity than ever before. It is not my purpose here either to discuss the decisions that have created a consumer society and to dispute the ideology behind it, or to question whether indeed it has been the demands of the market that create most technological advance.[5] Instead, I discuss the phenomenon of consumerism as it affects our consciousness and our unconscious, and shapes our desires and sense of ourselves, our aspirations, priorities and notions of what constitute reward: in short, our values.

The 1960s saw a rebellion against consumerism across the Western world. First the Beats and then the Hippies— the first generation of children to grow up in the prosperity following the Second World War—articulated a rejection of consumption as a *raison d'être* or as a genuine or reliable source of satisfaction. Their rebellion became subsumed under a more explicitly political movement throughout the United States and Western Europe. Subsequent responses to the consumer society over the last decade have been in contrast less anticonsumerist, more selective and specifically consumerist.[6] By and large consumerism, being able to buy the products in the market, be it clothes, fine wine or personal computers, is felt to be an important aspect of life and something worth working for. The objects that we consume become in turn invested with a power quite beyond their raw material and the social relations of production they embody.

There is a curious disjuncture between the labor process and the resulting object. The object, rather than being valued either as the expression of that labor process or for its usefulness, frequently takes on an altogether different meaning. It becomes invested with human values of status, power, wealth and sexuality. Acquisition of an object confers on its owner a kind of status, albeit a somewhat transitory one. There is a collective sense about the meaning of a specific object or group of objects. Inanimate things become both signposts for how to read people and vehicles of self-expression for the owners. They are immediate identity badges which convey (and at times attempt to conceal) information about class, gender, ethnicity (frequently), style and so on. For example, waves of immigrant workers have used clothing as a way to establish an American identity even when they have not yet acquired the English language. The use of objects in this way and the exalted role they play have profound consequences for our relations to ourselves:

Goods become actors in the pages of catalogs and in store displays. As customers, with free time from the activities of production, are increasingly invited to be admiring spectators, the social process of consumption [draws] upon the imagery of royalty, of religion, of magic to elaborate its atmosphere of promise.[7]

In contemporary America, consuming and being a good consumer is a highly regarded value. In the United Kingdom the situation is more complex. The economic logic pursued by recent governments, and the restructuring of capital,[8] has created tension in a society struggling to free itself from an ideological puritanism of denial historically promulgated as a good for those outside the aristocracy and the haute bourgeoisie. An economy caught between de-industrialization and a consumer-oriented industry finds itself with a population schooled in pre-consumerist values of thrift, conservation and a search for meaning in community and spirituality. (The resulting discomfort has created a kind of schizophrenic response—consumerism is good if you can afford it.) Because of the longer history of mass involvement in consumerism in the United States, this same search for value and meaning in life has taken a different turn there. Consumerism has been a way to partake in community, to be a good citizen, almost a good American. The golden arches of McDonald's hamburger franchises and of the Shoprite supermarket chain, reproduce in the architectural image the church of yesteryear. We enter them both to give and receive the blessing of a consumer society.

Within the new theology an interesting development from preconsumerist production and the consumer economy is the way in which the function of the human body has changed. Increasingly, because of automation on the one hand and the export of labor-intensive industry to Southeast Asia on the other, a generation of American and British youth is growing up fundamentally divorced from seeing their bodies as contributors to physical production, and beginning to regard them rather as instruments for active consumption. In other words, Westerners are experiencing an increasingly less physical relation to the wealth of the society in which they live. This alienation increases a general mystification as to how the available goods are actually produced. Quixotically, the avenue offered out of this particular alienation is the involvement in further or more intense consumption. A cycle of alienated buying is thus energized. But at the same time as this profoundly non-personal, non-physical relation to the market pertains, we are offered our bodies back, although on different terms.

Women's bodies have come to be used as titillating palliatives in the forging of a society whose economic rationale is consumption. Commodities from cars to Cokes to chemicals are displayed with young women close by signaling availability and sexuality. The alienated commodity becomes more desirable once washed with human attribution. In other words, the sexuality of women's bodies becomes split off and reattached to a whole host of commodities reflective of a consumer culture. Cars, Cokes and centrifuges become a form of sexuality, a means of access to one's own and/or another's body. In being perceived as the "uncontrollable" factor, sexuality asserts and bestows humanity on both the specific product and the process of consuming. Sexuality is felt to be real in some fundamental way. Related to passion, sensuality, love and the irrational, it is simultaneously seen and presented as a point beyond the control of the machine and commercialism, while being packaged as a purchasable commodity. Sex becomes something appropriated as a by-product of consuming. The car makes the man sexy and he "gets the girl."

The disjuncture discussed earlier between the labor process and the commodity is sadly paralleled in the overall societal attitude towards sexuality, and more especially women's bodies. They are, to both women and men, objects of alienation, fascination and desire. Chapter 4 will deal with women's body-images in greater detail and suggest historical and psychological reasons for the taking-up of its exploitation in this manner. For the present, I wish to draw attention to the sexual aspect of women's physicality used in the service of bridging the enormous gulf between the process of production and the act of consumption. This has consequences for the commoditized way in which we think of human sexuality and inevitably has an impact on our notions of femininity. Almost all current representations of sexuality have focused on women's bodies as the site of contemporary sexuality. (As homosexuality becomes more visible so we are seeing the emergence of male bodies and new imagery, but this recent development has not as yet affected the culture in general.)

Many commentators[9] have written extensively about the change in labor process or the phenomenon of alienation in capitalist society, but they have failed to take into account the crucial role of women's bodies in conveying the cultural hegemony of marketplace values. The Frankfurt School[10] has focused on sexuality and sublimation and in so doing has opened the way to the present argument. Yet only in feminist discourse has the point been made that a particular fantasized and *gendered* version of sexuality is the substitute for other kinds of contact.

As participants in a consumer society we fashion our needs in relation to existing possibilities. Our imagination is necessarily circumscribed by the context in which it is nurtured. Thus our notions of our capabilities and our very responses are shaped by the prevailing views of our society. For women themselves, the body has become a commodity within the marketplace or, as I have suggested elsewhere, their own commodity, the object with which they negotiate the world.[11] The multitude of images and meanings that women's bodies represent forms a part of each individual woman's relationship with her own and other women's bodies. It would be hard to argue that women have an unmediated or purely physical relation to their bodies due to the immense amount of cultural significance they carry. There exists no "pure" relationship under the weight of cultural innuendo, for each woman's relationship with her body is constructed within a cultural nexus. Thus each woman has to find a way of being with and in her body that expresses both her oneness with the culture and her individuality. But this imperative itself is problematic, as women are encouraged to see their bodies from the outside, as if they were commodities. Feminine perception is informed by a devastatingly fierce, visual acuity turned in on itself. It operates almost as a third eye.

A woman's experience of her own body stems from the interaction of two sources: first, how she believes it compares with the magnified images of women that surround her on billboards and on television, in movies, magazines and newspapers; and second, how she has come to relate to her body from early on in her life. In those instances in which a woman grows up with a reasonably good feeling about her own physicality, her body shape and female body functions, she may be able to temper the indignities and daily assault of a diet and "beauty" industry bent on creating body insecurity in women. She may be able to ignore or dismiss the onslaught. More often than not, however, a woman is unable to cast off those insistent images and they get under her skin. She is receptive to the messages proclaiming her body—this crucial commodity in her life—as deficient and in need of attention. Her inner feelings of discomfort seem to be temporarily relieved by the salvationary promises of the clothing, dieting and beauty industries, and she finds a certain solace in knowing that she can improve, that she can remake herself. The receptivity that women show (across class, ethnicity and through the generations) to the idea that their bodies are like

gardens—arenas for constant improvement and resculpting
—is rooted in a recognition of their bodies as commodities. A consumer society in which women's bodies perform the critical function of humanizing other products
while being presented as the ultimate commodity, creates
all sorts of body-image problems for women, both at the
level of distortion about their own and others' bodies, and
in creating a disjuncture from their bodies. To understand
further why a woman's body is so critical to her sense of
self, and how many themes are expressed in eating problems, we need to look at women's changing social role
during the last forty years.

The rise in anorexia is occurring in a population whose
ages range from fifteen to forty, with a vast cluster of
women in their late teens and twenties. The last forty
years have seen shifts in women's lives, in styles of
parenting, both at the level of parental obligation and of
expectations as to the roles that girl children and boy
children should assume. These shifts need to be explored
in order to understand the pressures of parenting and the
ensuing confusion which mothers, fathers and children
have experienced.

Parenting can often look or feel like a monolithic and
unchanging entity, and indeed there are constants in the
structure of parenting from one generation to the next, but
broad social changes have an impact on parenting so that
what is thought to constitute good parenting in one period
may differ markedly from one decade to the next. What is
especially interesting about the shape of parenting for those
raising children in the 1940s, 1950s and 1960s is the
dramatic social changes that occurred every few years. The
values with which these parents were themselves raised are
challenged by larger social forces, but the fashion in child-
rearing changes so rapidly that a new way of parenting
cannot be consolidated. The possibility of being consistent

and feeling confident that one is doing the right thing is an elusive goal amid the changing views of what form good parenting, and especially good mothering, should take. These changes create mothers insecure in their jobs. What is right now will be wrong tomorrow. What was done yesterday is criticized today. A kind of insecurity underlies the structure of parenting during this period and has an impact on the psychology of the children. As we shall see, anorexia becomes an understandable, if extreme, response to these shifts. It symbolizes a search for certainty and order in the face of tumult.

For a large number of women starting families during the Second World War, parenting was undertaken as a sole responsibility. Women who became pregnant when their husbands were on leave or before they were called up to fight, envisioned for themselves periods of single parenting that they hoped would end with the safe return of their spouses. Because women were required to run industries vital to the war effort in both the United States and England, the governments of those two countries provided round-the-clock nursery facilities for the care of the young in the cities. While parenting decisions would at first glance seem to fall exclusively on women, the existence of reliable day care centers for infants and young children, together with the collective spirit of survival that emerged during wartime, meant that parenting was a much less proprietary act. Much of a woman's energy went into working for the war effort, and for many people it was a time in which they developed undreamed-of skills and built a camaraderie around work, and a sense of importance as workers. Propaganda films, news reels and photostories depicted women's centrality to war work and the self-esteem a woman could gain through this valuable enterprise. It was thus quite a jolt when in 1945 the men returned from the war and a different message was beamed at women. Now the definition of what constituted essential female work shifted arenas. Motherhood and making a home—a baby in the nursery, a pie in the oven—were elevated to almost saintly proportions. Female ambition was to be replaced by the professional mother and home-maker, a job requiring more skills, time and input from other experts. Women were induced to put their consider-able energies into the household and to seek their satisfac-tions from the knowledge that they were good homemakers and mothers.

Numerous experts materialized to guide women in this new—albeit according to the ideology—biologically des-tined and therefore almost holy role. Popular magazines dumped "Rosie the Riveter" and took up the slogan of "Give us back our wives and sweethearts." The movies were full of happy families with mother contentedly at home. Meanwhile women's magazines and radio shows of the period started to discuss the dire effects of maternal absence on the mental health of children, and the nurseries were shut in an attempt to encourage women to take up their destined role.

A burgeoning number of experts in child-rearing materi-alized, counseling women first this way, now that way, on how to carry out this role correctly. Through books, talks and magazine articles, they disseminated their ideas on the rightness first of bottle-feeding, then of breast-feeding; the necessity of scheduled feeding; the necessity of demand feeding; the correctness of disciplining; of being liberal; the importance of hugging crying children; and the importance of not indulging crying children.[12] In addition women were counseled about *their* importance in the career development of their husbands. A wife's sensitivity to her husband's needs was essential to his progress. She would find satisfaction through his success and through the identification of his needs as *her* needs. The family became invested as the haven from the world of competition at work, the natural site for the caring of preschool children, and the desired domain of women.

This jump-shift in women's lives was not without emotional cost to women and families despite the enormous ideological resources that were brought to bear on everyone's consciousness. Many women continued to work out of economic necessity but were faced with feelings of guilt about not being good enough mothers. Those women who wished to pursue work outside the home but were not dependent on outside income, battled with both a kind of discrimination on the job and internal questioning about whether or not they were damaging their husbands and children. For many women confinement at home meant no independent money and an economic dependency that created attitudes of subservience in women (and superiority in men), and in effect devalued the work they were doing in the home. The strong, capable women who worked and raised their children during the war were relegated to the world of the home and familial concern.

While white women were excluded from a satisfying social existence outside the home, black women were receiving a setback with a twist. The ideological picture of life in the American black family (mainly created by white people) gave us mythological pictures of the black woman's ability to cope with work, child-rearing, grandparenting and so on. However, these images were promoted not with the aim of honoring the often heroic efforts of these women but with the intent of criticizing those very same women for emasculating the black man. Thus the black woman found herself blamed for unemployment, poverty and the breakup of family life.[13]

Cross-culturally, children were the province of women. It was a woman's role to produce healthy children with psyches well-balanced according to the latest psychologi-

cal theory. A version of Freud's work became widely
disseminated at this time and this, together with studies
coming out of the orphanages set up during the Second
World War,[14] gave rise to an intense concentration on the
mother's centrality to the mental health of children. Women
were encouraged to spend maximum time and creative
energy relating to their preschool children, and the phenomenon of childhood and its developmental phases
became instituted.

For nearly all women, the structural isolation of their
daily lives discouraged a free discussion and exploration of
the conditions of their existence. There was a kind of
knowing and inevitable quality to the dissatisfaction. Wom-
en's lives were often disappointing, frustrating and limiting, and women became skilled at comforting each other
around the kitchen table and taking the sting out of the
confined lives they led. Expeditions to hastily constructed
shopping malls and high streets purported to offer women
some kind of temporary outlet and fleeting feelings of
important decision-making over which goods to purchase.
However, these temporary distractions could not still the
disquiet inside so many women or provide the kind of
satisfaction the goods seemed to promise.

This is the situation that pertained until the mid-1960s.
It was the world whose consequences Betty Friedan described so vividly in *Feminine Mystique*:[15] a world of
thwarted ambition and domestic frustration for women, of
dissatisfaction that was intangible or, to use Friedan's
words, "the problem with no name." Part of what characterized homemaking at this time was a denial that it might
not satisfy all women. Women whose discontent came to
the surface were pathologized. Not accepting one's place
meant a trip to the general practitioner or psychiatrist for
Valium,[16] or therapy to adjust better. (Those who could
not adjust became the victims of psychiatric abuse.[17])

Women whose discomfort hovered around the surface blamed themselves for their own failure to cope with the requirements of their social role. At the same time they became the butt of a whole host of jokes about Jewish mothers and nagging wives. The frustration of their truncated lives sought an outlet in a preoccupation with their children's or husband's success.

The children especially were designated as the mother's objects. Mother was to make them perfect and they would represent her accomplishment. Sons and daughters became both the mother's objects and her raison d'être. It was not simply that mothers had the responsibility of raising the children according to the values of the time, but that being the recipients of her most intense attention, they were to gratify her in the world. In the case of boy children, this meant fulfilling themselves in ways forbidden to her (hence the edge associated with the utterance "my son the doctor"). As regards girl children, a mother's desires tended to be somewhat contradictory—"Be like me,' "Don't be like me.' In both instances there was enormous pressure in the mother–child relationship, and a child's success could never be enough, for it could not address women's needs for self-expression.

The frustration that was evident in many women's lives surfaced dramatically in the late 1960s and early 1970s with the emergence of the Women's Liberation Movement bursting with an energy to rethink all categories of female experience. Parenting and mothering were among the topics that consciousness-raising groups took up, and for the women who were concurrently mothering, the insights gained in such groups demanded a reappraisal of family life and especially the concept of the all-providing wife and mother. The resentment that had seethed beneath the surface or been somatized in countless ways, was examined, and women were able to recognize the social basis of many of the difficulties they had previously experienced and interpreted as evidence of individual failure.

For many women such insights were translated into immediate changes on the home front and in domestic relations, leading in many cases to a return to higher education, seeking work outside the home, setting up of day care centers for preschool children, and so on. The pioneers of such changes had an impact on how all women came to see themselves, and the idea of work outside the home once more became a generally respectable and desired goal. During the 1970s and until the present time there has been a gradual entry of women into job categories previously closed to them, and both women and men have been confronted with the necessity of restructuring parenting and child care arrangements.

In the vast majority of cases it is still the woman who conceives herself as having the primary responsibility for providing the custodial care of children during the day and arranging substitutes for herself if she is planning to be unavailable. But even though these responsibilities continue to be gender-linked, that does not preclude the impact that this shift has created on women's self-image and styles of mothering, and subsequently on the mother–child dyad. Thus since the Second World War most families have experienced changes in the kind of parenting practiced and received, and the mothers within those families have been subject to several changes in their social role. Mothers who may have been intensely involved at a particular period of a child's life have begun to put some of their energy, hopes and ambitions elsewhere. For many women this new option has created unexpectedly complicated feelings: elements of guilt and confusion co-mingle with the feelings of liberation and growing self-esteem. The feelings that a woman has about herself and the possibilities she sees ahead for her children have their impact in the mother–child relationship and hence in the developing psychology of the child.

Women who in early married life anticipated having jobs outside the home, were then discouraged and only recently rediscovered that desire legitimized, will inevitably have related somewhat inconsistently towards their children, especially their daughters, both at the level of expectations and in terms of what they themselves projected and modeled about the actualities and possibilities in women's lives. This shifting in a mother's own sense of her self and the possibilities she envisions for her children can be extremely confusing for the child. By the same token, daughters with desires to extend the definition of the female social role but who were brought up by mothers apparently contented with it, experience a profusion of troubling feelings including disloyalty, abandonment and guilt—feelings which may well not find acceptable expression within the family.

The post-Second World War period, then, is a particularly fraught one in the history of parenting, as it is characterized by these shifts in the definition of what constitutes good child-rearing. If the mother does not know what to hold on to in the social roller-coaster ride of this period, even less does the daughter who experiences a world with few enduring values, little consistency and a paucity of control. The thread of this heritage is visible in the action of the anorectic. The rigidity of the syndrome is a symbolic attempt to forge a consistency where little exists, to provide a knowable, reliable way of being that can withstand the demand for change.

We turn now to the mother–daughter relationship to understand in finer detail how the pressures on contemporary parenting affect the construction of the psychology of femininity—a psychology that creates a fertile ground for the development of the whole range of eating problems

and body-image difficulties that so many women experience.
Before detailing the structure of the mother–daughter relationship, I wish to stress how time- and culturally-specific
the observations I am making are. In other words, the
particular tensions that are presently folded into the mother–
daughter relationship largely arise from the broad social
forces I have outlined above. These conditions for child-
rearing are quite different from those existing before or
during the Second World War, in which a family network
and the realities of community were present. Similarly, in
the nineteenth century, there was far less attention to the
phenomenon of childhood. Where it existed it was confined to certain sections of the upper middle class. What is
especially remarkable about parenting in the post-Second
World War period is the swings and shifts in ideas of what
good mothering meant. In previous periods, styles of parenting extended over several decades, and the mother–
daughter relationships in history were less subject to the
pressures of the latest panel of "experts" on child development heralding the correct way of parenting. But that said,
it is nevertheless possible to generalize about the structure
of the contemporary mother–daughter relationship.

Feminist theorists[18] have located the family as the trans-
mitter of an inferior psychology of women. It is within the
family structure, and in particular the mother–daughter
relationship, that a girl first learns the outlines of her social
role. This process occurs simultaneously with her developing sense of self.[19] In our culture, mothers are responsible
for the psychological and social development of infants
from the biological category of sex to the social category
of gender.[20] In other words, a mother directs her children's
development in gender-appropriate ways, both at the level
of socialization and in terms of the formation of psychic
structure. The impact of this social demand on the mother–
daughter relationship is profound.

The mother–daughter relationship is inevitably an ambivalent one, for the mother who herself lives a circumscribed life in patriarchy, has the unenviable task of directing her daughter to take up the very same position that she has occupied. Explicitly as well as unconsciously she psychologically prepares her daughter to accept the strictures that await her in womanhood. She needs to do this so that her daughter is not cast as a misfit. Of course there is a broad range of behaviors and activities that mothers indicate are acceptable, but the construction of femininity is bounded by fundamental social laws that delineate the parameters of a woman's life.

For a young woman today, developing femininity successfully requires meeting three basic demands. The first of these is that she must defer to others, the second that she must anticipate and meet the needs of others, and the third, that she must seek self-definition through connection with another. The consequences of these requirements frequently mean that in denying themselves, women are unable to develop an authentic sense of their needs or a feeling of entitlement for their desires. Preoccupied with others' experience and unfamiliar with their own needs, women come to depend on the approval of those to whom they give. The imperative of affiliation, the cultural demand that a woman must define herself through association with another, means that many aspects of self are under-developed, producing insecurity and a shaky sense of self. Under the competent carer who gives to the world lives a hungry, deprived and needy little girl who is unsure and ashamed of her desires and wants.[21] So the social requirements and their consequences make for a psychology marked by two essential features. There exist in all women, to some degree, two deeply internalized taboos (which are socially reinforced). One is against the expression of dependency needs, and the other is the taboo against initiating.[22] Most people are keenly aware of how women's initiations are discouraged and frowned upon. A woman who is opinionated, determined, or directly lets her needs be known is frequently denigrated or grudgingly described as pushy and aggressive. Less recognized is how forcefully girls and women repress their needs for dependence and nurturance. The situation is complicated by the fact that simultaneous with the covert instruction to curtail one's needs are two seemingly paradoxical injunctions. Firstly, girls are encouraged to display a range of dependent and deferential behavior such as appearing "not to know" and requiring aid in such matters as changing a light bulb (in order to give life to the ideological dictum about men's superior strength and women's weakness); secondly, they are guided to convert their own wish to be attended to into caring and responding to others. In this way women's true dependency needs are deeply buried and inevitably experienced with shame and distress. Their needs, thwarted and unmet, go underground. A psychological consequence of the suppression of women's desires for both dependency gratification and autonomy is that women do not feel good within themselves. They feel unentitled, they feel wrong. They constantly search to feel all right, and the approval of others temporarily quiets the uneasy feelings inside.

This is the psychology that women bring to mothering. In relating to a baby girl whose needs are obvious and pressing, the mother's own life experience of containing her dependency needs and restricting her initiating desires is stimulated in particularly painful ways. The role of mothering includes directing a daughter in gender-appropriate ways, and just as a mother cannot set up false expectations about adult life for her daughter, so in their relationship the mother knowingly as well as unconsciously distills the social laws. The mother–daughter relationship itself becomes marked by a kind of rejection of the daughter's dependency needs, as well as her desires for autonomy. The daughter's needs stir up her mother's own unmet needs, and arouse in her a range of conscious and unconscious responses which produce an inconsistency in her behavior. For example, sometimes the mother can accept the babyishness of her daughter, her whining and whimpering, the fussiness that seems to have no obvious cause. She attends to her and through the contact conveys a sense that the little girl can be helped through a period in which she feels out of sorts. At other times, though, or even within the same specific incident, the mother suddenly finds her daughter's neediness irrepressibly irritating and annoying. She tries to curtail it, frequently by diverting the little girl into taking her into account: "That's enough now, mummy has a headache," or by encouraging her to put away her distress: "Come on, don't be such a baby now."

These kinds of action fueled by the mother's own difficulties with the topic of neediness have the effect of confusing the little girl. Sometimes her needs are acceptable and sometimes not. She becomes uneasy about expressing them, which in turn makes her unsure of her needs, ashamed of them, and eventually produces in her a general feeling of insecurity. In addition she becomes quite clinging as this insecurity leads her to seek fairly constant assurance.

This clingingness may be unthinkingly and unconsciously encouraged by the mother's other actions. As the little girl makes tentative steps towards "independent" activity such as climbing stairs or crawling out of the room, the mother may transmit her anxiety about these activities in particular ways to a girl child. She may chase after her or convey a

sense of the danger on the staircase so that whereas a boy
child may be encouraged—"Come on, you can do it . . .
now try the next one, and the next . . . clever boy"—the
little girl may hear, "Now be very careful, not too
fast . . . don't slip . . . be careful." I have perhaps over-
emphasized the different words that might be used in
teaching a boy child and a girl child respectively to climb
stairs, but I do this as a device to draw attention to a
difference that is frequently conveyed at a nonverbal level.
The boy rushing towards the staircase may engender an
exasperated look in a worried mother, but she will quickly
smile and encourage him to complete the task. She trans-
mits the idea that these kinds of physical endeavor are
right for him to master, just as later climbing up trees
and over railroad tracks is part of being a boy. The girl
rushing to the staircase engenders more panic because
her physicality is in general to be restrained. The worried
mother stands and frets over whether she can make it up
and down the stairs. She may not be able to convey the
same confidence in mastery of such a skill that she does
to a boy.

For these two reasons, then—the mother's failure actively to encourage a girl's initiatives, and her inability to
provide the daughter with adequate or consistent gratification of early dependency needs—the little girl comes to
have difficulty in the process of psychological separation
which starts at about six months and continues through to
the third year of life, for she still needs an experience of
consistent nurturance. The capacity to experience oneself
as a separate person, as a subject (to individuate), rests on
the gratification of early dependency needs.[23] Thus the
developmental phase of separation—individuation is scarred.
The mother is reluctant to let her daughter go (for the
mother herself may be merged with her daughter out of her
own lack of having a separated self), and the daughter

herself has not yet embodied a sufficient sense of self to separate.

There is evidence to suggest that these taboos on female desire and the structure "not to expect too much" is expressed in the feeding and holding aspects of the mother–daughter relationship. In a study of Italian infants, Lezine[24] reports marked differences in the feeding patterns and the feeding ambience based on gender. Sixty-six percent of the girls were breast-fed as compared to 99 percent of the boys. Girls were weaned significantly earlier than boys and in general, time alloted to feeding activities was distinctively less for girls than for boys. The same discrepancy was observed in relation to patterns of holding. Girl infants were held for shorter periods of time than boys.[25] Informal reports by child analysts and developmental psychologists confirm this kind of difference (even where the issue is not bottle versus breasts, but time and contact). These observations point to a continuity between the early feeding patterns of girls and accepted feeding patterns in adult women. The earlier behavior is in a sense preparative. Just as adult women are counseled to curb their desires for food in the interest of current aesthetics, so girl children become accustomed early on to getting less. Thus the very first relationship that a girl experiences is one in which she takes in a powerful message of denial—of emotional nurturance—the desire for autonomy, and in relation to the restraint of physical appetite. These broad statements are not intended to hold exactly true for each mother–daughter relationship, but rather to delineate the parameters of that first most crucial relationship in a girl's life.

As girls enter adolescence, the issues that are still live from the earlier developmental phase of separation–individuation become re-evoked in a new and dramatic form. The struggle for an identity separate from the family is made on fairly shaky foundations. Detachment from the family and realignment with peers involves tension and distress. Just as the earlier separation is desired at one level, the wish to stay close and "protected" within the well-known psychic ambience, is in conflict with the desire for separation and autonomy. Lambley[26] discusses how parents of anorectic children interfere in the child's attempt to establish normal peer relations which are an important component in the building of pre-adult identity. The parents are inclined to criticize the daughter's choice of friends or group out of the need to keep the child close to home and exclusively involved in the emotional life of the family.

The insecurity felt by the adolescent, the fear of separation from the family, and the wish for acceptance in the new critical peer environment produce in girls an overwhelming desire to conform. In addition, the dramatic physical changes that occur in puberty rock the young woman's already tenuous psychic foundations. Her body is changing without her intervention and the outcome of these changes is unpredictable. They may exemplify her lack of control or her capacity to make things come out her way. Insecurity in oneself becomes transposed into an insecurity in relation to one's body.

During adolescence, the mother–daughter relationship loses none of its intensity or ambivalence. A mother's feelings about her daughter's sexual development are experienced within the mother–daughter relationship. As a mother has herself lived with the pressure to have a fashionably attractive body, she is unlikely to have felt relaxed and confident in her body. If she has battled with a "weight problem" for many years, she may visit this problem on her adolescent daughter by becoming watchful of what she eats and preoccupied with her changing body contours. She does this with the best of intentions, but her observations are frequently experienced as intrusive. Alternatively many mothers, threatened by their daughter's developing sexuality, are unable to welcome and legitimate the exciting body changes that the young woman is going through. And so the daughter seeks confirmation and understanding outside the family in the bosom of her girlfriends and the magazines written explicitly for the teenage market. One thing that adolescent magazines uniformly preach as the solution to the crises of adolescence is dieting and weight control. Young women read that dieting is both the passport to teenage life and the answer to a whole host of named and unnamed problems. The psychic insecurity is now addressed by the modern panacea—diet and control. Thus girls are initiated into the adult relationship they are to have with their bodies. Be vigilant, control your desires for food (and incidentally for sex), be frightened of your body, it is always waiting to let you down.

The adolescent girl is learning to develop a split between her body and her self. There is, if you like, the embryo of a psychosomatic split. Her body is rapidly being presented to her and being perceived by her as an artefact, albeit an essential one, both divorced from and yet reflective of who and what she is. What do I mean by this paradoxical statement? As we have seen, a woman tends to view her body almost as one removed. Her survey of it is undertaken with more or less anxiety. She looks at her image in the mirror with a distance and the question of whether it (that is, she) is acceptable.[27] The standard she applies reflects her internalization of cultural values. She measures how far from the projected norm she is, she fantasizes the benefits that arise from conforming. Her body is a statement about her and the world and her statement about her position in the world. Living within prescribed boundaries, women's bodies become the vehicle for a whole range of expressions that have no other medium.[28] The body, offered as a woman's ticket into society (i.e. through it she meets a mate and thus her sexuality and her role is legitimated), becomes her mouthpiece. In her attempts to conform or reject contemporary ideals of femininity, she uses the weapon so often directed against her. She speaks with her body.

In the next chapter we shall see how these themes are expressed more directly vis-à-vis food and the feeding relationship. For the moment, I wish to emphasize the shape of the mother–daughter relationship in general, and its impact on the developing psychology of girls and women. For while anorexia and other eating and body-image problems do not affect all women, there is a continuity in all women's experience which makes them vulnerable to such problems. While some of this vulnerability, as we shall see, is certainly due to the central part food plays in women's social role, it rests on this very relation to the psychology just described—a psychology that tends to deny women's feelings of entitlement, initiation and nurturance, creating defense structures that embody a discomfort with oneself. Anorexia becomes the quintessential expression of that discomfort with oneself—it is an extreme manifestation of the denial of selfhood.

## NOTES

1. John Sours in *Starving to Death in a Sea of Objects* (New York, 1980) points out that there is a sixteenth-century report of anorexia nervosa in Genoa and an early seventeenth-century report in France. The nosology of anorexia nervosa dates to Sir William Gull in England in 1868 and Dr. E.C. Lesegue in France in 1873. There has been a certain amount of unease with the inaccurate use of terminology but it has now come into popular and technical use so widely that a more accurate term seems unlikely to be adopted.
2. Crisp, A.H., Palmer, R.L. and Kalucy, R.S., "How Common is Anorexia Nervosa? A Prevalence Study," *British Journal of Psychiatry*, 128 (1976), 549-54.
3. Chodorow, N., *The Reproduction of Mothering. Psychoanalysis and the Sociology of Gender* (Berkeley, 1978); Dinnerstein, D., *The Mermaid and The Minotaur: Sexual Arrangements and Human Malaise* (New York, 1976); Eichenbaum, L. and

Orbach, S., *Understanding Women: A Feminist Psychoanalytic Approach* (New York, 1983).

4. Bruch, H., *Eating Disorders; Obesity, Anorexia Nervosa, and the Person Within* (New York, 1973); Palazzoli, M. Selvini, *Self-Starvation. From the Intrapsychic to the Transpersonal Approach to Anorexia Nervosa* (London, 1974); Orbach, S., *Fat is a Feminist Issue* (London, 1978); Orbach, S., *Fat is a Feminist Issue II* (London, 1983).

5. As opposed to the manipulation of it or the offspring of the military.

6. See, for example, the work of Ralph Nader or the response of communities of "consumers" to proposed nuclear power stations.

7. Ewan, E. and Ewan, S., *Channels of Desire* (New York, 1982), p. 70.

8. Friend, A. and Metcalf, A., *Slump City* (London, 1981).

9. Braverman, H., *Labor and Monopoly Capital* (New York, 1978); Turkel, S., *Working* (New York, 1974); Garson, B., *All The Live Long Day* (New York, 1975).

10. Marcuse, H., *Eros and Civilization* (Boston, 1955).

11. Orbach, *op. cit.* (1978); Orbach, *op. cit.* (1982).

12. Lasch, C., *The Culture of Narcissism* (New York, 1979).

13. Moynihan, D., *The Negro Family: The Case for National Action* (US Department of Labor, Washington DC, 1965).

14. Spitz, R., *The First Year of Life: A Psychoanalytic Study of Normal and Deviant Development of Object Relations* (New York, 1965).

15. Friedan, B., *The Feminine Mystique* (New York, 1963).

16. Valium (diazepam) was introduced in 1963.

17. Chesler, P., *Women and Madness* (New York, 1972).

18. Mitchell, J., *Women's Estate* (New York, 1973).

19. Money, J. and Erhardt, A., *Man and Woman, Boy and Girl: The Differentiation and Dimorphism of Gender Identity from Conception to Maturity* (Baltimore, 1973).

20. Eichenbaum and Orbach, *op. cit.*

21. Eichenbaum, L. and Orbach, S., *What Do Women Want?* (London, 1983).

22. *Ibid.*

23. Fairbairn, W.R.D., *Psychoanalytic Studies of the Personality* (London, 1952).

24. As cited by Belotti, E.G., in *Little Girls* (New York, 1977).

25. *Ibid.*

26. Lambley, P., *How to Survive Anorexia* (London, 1983).

27. Berger, J., *Ways of Seeing* (London, 1972).

28. Orbach, *op. cit.* (1978).

# 3   Starving Amidst Plenty

The aftermath of the Second World War ushered in significant changes in the production and distribution of foodstuffs throughout Western Europe and the United States. After rationing ceased in the early 1950s, it seemed as though food was plentiful, abundant and reasonably cheap. The notion grew up that the West had eliminated starvation, and although there was much evidence to the contrary, and gross inequities in the distribution of food, the belief in the idea of plenitude was dominant and was to lead to a series of consequences in the meaning of food in everyday life.

In most people's experience there were vast changes in food delivery. Refrigerators, already a part of the American kitchen, became commonplace in British and European households, thus eliminating the need for daily shopping. Several days' food in the refrigerator implied more availability than a well-stocked pantry. The growth of supermarkets with their rows and rows of dairy products, canned goods, meats, condiments, bakery goods, vegetables, fruits and staples, brought a large display of foods into everybody's range. Few people could leave a supermarket without buying more than they intended, and the kitchen—often the center of the home—contained an ever wider variety of foods.

Although there are variations in cultural practices in relation to food—stereotypes include the American kitchen crammed with every kind of snack food from tacos to popcorn; the Italian mama kneading the pasta; the endless cups of tea around the kitchen table in England; or the rigidity of the French bourgeois kitchen—in many families the kitchen and mealtimes provided the emotional hub of the household. Even where convention defied the stereotype, for instance in England, where for large sections of the adult population the draw of the pub meant that Dad was frequently missing from the kitchen or dining table, the *idea* of home life was entwined with the cozy kitchen, food preparation and mealtimes.

The abundance of food now visible in the kitchen was by no means restricted to home life. Throughout the United States the ubiquitous franchised eating place sprang up in every town, bringing economic life to the previously barren highway and creating the "strip," that brightly lit mile of brand-name eateries and gasoline stations. Standardized food could be found in almost every price range, from the cheap hamburger with all the trimmings to stylized "gourmet" restaurants offering the cuisines of different nations. For those offended by the pseudo-community of interest that the franchises and the supermarkets purported to represent, a new lease on life occurred with speciality food shops, farmers' markets and chef-proprietor restaurants. Both the health food phenomenon which started in the 1960s and the interest in *nouvelle cuisine* in the 1970s were in some sense anti-corporate rebellions against hi-tech food production and delivery. They were attempts to make personal statements through food: "You are what you eat." This statement was to be taken up with vigor by those people who wanted food to express their individuality, their uniqueness, their personality.

During the last twenty-five years the high visibility of food and its apparent abundance has created a cleavage in our perceptions of it. More than ever, and for more people than ever before, food is no longer felt to be simply the adequate response to physical hunger. Changes in ways of relating to food have mimicked certain aspects of the fashion industry. Food has become high style itself. How, what and where one eats is meant to, and does, convey aspects of self to the wider community. Food has taken on attributes of a status symbol, very like the car. For many people, especially those with some surplus income in the professional and business middle class, it has become a *divertissement*, a form of entertainment and expression of disdain for mass production. Partaking of the *sushi* prepared by a Japanese chef with seven years' training in cutting fish is a contemporary stand-in for the hand-finished cars available to increasingly fewer people. There is inevitably a frantic rush to get into the latest restaurant discovered by the food critics, and the food eaten under such conditions is as much an expression of status as a culinary experience. A whole vocabulary for food *aficionados* has developed, and being "out of fashion" with food preferences is a sign of gaucheness and ineptitude.

In England, the disdain noted in the previous chapter in relation to consumerism in general, is paralleled in relation to food. There is a tension between those who perceive food as an aesthetic statement and those who continue to hold a fairly utilitarian attitude towards it. There is thus some restraint on what many see as indulgence, but the same economic forces that create the franchises, speciality shops and supermarkets throughout the United States are ensuring an increasingly high visibility of food in the UK too. In other Western European countries, a genuine love of food, and the hospitality it represents, has been less eroded, and there is more continuity in people's relationship to food and the institutions of food delivery than in the UK and the USA.

Despite such dissimilarities as exist in the Western world in relation to food, and the recent emergence of food as a status symbol or form of fashion—influences that we shall see bear directly on the emergence of eating problems in general and anorexia specifically—underlying these developments are more basic responses which human beings tend to have towards food and which stem from its original and highly central role in all of our lives.

For all of us, food is the most basic medium of communication from the first day of our lives. In the cocooned world of the baby, attention to hunger is imbued with a kaleidoscope of emotional nuances. The feeding ambience provides many things. First there is the obvious point: the baby cries out of hunger and is fed. It is reassured that the discomfort caused by hunger can be relieved. This in turn creates a confidence that desires that seem to arise from inside can be met, for feelings of satisfaction and contentment follow the expression of the infant's need.

At first it is thought that the baby perceives this as a rather magical process, with the breast or bottle appearing coincidentally with its desires, but gradually, as the baby seems to develop an awareness of her or himself and its surroundings, it can feel its own impact (usually described as the omnipotent phase) and see how another is being responsive towards it. The feeding relationship resonates far more deeply than simply at the level of physical satisfaction. The process of feeding sets up a whole tableau of feelings that affect not just our relationship with food, but our experience of closeness and intimacy. For feeding always takes place within an intimate context, usually that of mother or female mother substitute and child. It is the primary form of relating for the first few months of life when the baby alternates between sleep and hunger. It is a physical exchange between two people, it requires a getting to know on both sides: the baby is required to accommodate to the breast and/or the bottle, the mother to respond to the baby's pace, the amount it wants, and when it wants to be fed.

The mother has much of the responsibility of setting up the eating ambience, and the feelings she brings to it inevitably form an important part of what occurs within it. For some mothers, feeding, especially the feeding of an infant, is a blissful time, when she feels tremendous pleasure and satisfaction at being needed and able to give in this way. She loves the intimate connection with her baby and feels a contentment in being able to be a provider. The ease with which she approaches feeding times is communicated to the infant, who takes her or his time to adjust, confident that the breast and the holding is there when needed. At first the baby may well not know that the object which brings satisfaction is outside itself. Feeding time is thought of as a state of being in a period of wakefulness and arousal for the infant, who soon slips back into the sleeping state.

As the infant develops, so what happens in the feeding changes. The baby develops a sense of the breast and the mother's body as outside itself. It becomes used to expecting the contact in the feeding situation and looks forward to this form of comfort, knowing that it will not be precipitately withdrawn. Sometimes the baby is thought to hallucinate its presence when it requires the kind of soothing experienced in the feeding relationship. The baby begins to play with the breast or the bottle, gradually developing an interest in other foods that are around. The feeding relationship has to grow as the baby develops. Its desire for, or the parents' decision to give it, a wider range of food, means an adjustment for both sides in the relationship. A mother attached to giving a baby her breast may feel a loss when instead she provides solid foods with a spoon. It is not just that the baby is taking in something that is not hers, but that she no longer holds the baby in her arms when feeding it. The physical closeness associated with feeding departs. She is face to face with a baby in a chair. The shift to solid food represents steps towards the baby's mastery of new skills and interest in the world beyond the breast. This can be an exciting time, but it can also be extremely trying for the mother. She may experience the baby's new ''independence'' as a loss or a relief or a mixture of both. She may feel guilty that she no longer provides all. She may wish to keep the baby on the breast longer, as it contributes to her own feelings of value and extends the early intimacy she felt with the infant. All such reactions are entirely within the range of most mothers who cannot help but feel ambivalent about the changes that occur constantly in the feeding relationship.

Feeding times may shift from the blissful connected states to a time of play where the baby toys with food, examines it, spits it out, gurgles for more and so on. These goings-on are one of the ways the baby is beginning to express itself; it is extending the repertoire of activities that occur in what has been an essentially pleasing situation. The coyness, eagerness or straightforward playfulness it displays during feeding times are some of the first expressions of the developing personality of the child. The switch to solid food may signal the start of working out issues around control. The baby's refusal or playfulness may distress the mother and she in turn may become frustrated and edgy—devoid of the patience she brought earlier to the feeding relationship. The mother has the job of constantly shifting to mirror her baby's evolving wishes and needs. Some women find this quite easy to do and follow a kind of parallel development with the growing child; as the child shows more motor skills and "independence," so the mother's interests turn outside the nursery environment. Other mothers find the shifts disruptive and hard to implement. For many women the feeding ambience is rich with sensual intimacy, while others approach feeding with a desire to be efficient and do a competent job. Obviously the attitude the mother brings is communicated to the baby, and as it is the fundamental way in which the person is first introduced to food and eating, it resonates in each person's relationship with food throughout life.

From the first days of life to the end of their days, most people experience a similar constant in relation to food. The eating of food occurs in a social context, one in which nine times out of ten it is a woman who prepares and serves it. For although many men now cook, both professionally and for pleasure, the vast majority of meals are purchased, prepared and served by women. Our earliest memories of food being associated with women are reinforced daily.

Women's influence is felt in every area of family life and psychological development, but nowhere so poignantly as in the arena of food. A mother provides breakfast, take-away lunch, dinner and snacks according to a thought-out balancing of children's desires and nutritional requirements with the family's particular economic position. A mother's presence is always implicit in food. It is almost as if food, in its many and varied forms, becomes a representation of the mother. From the child's point of view, the essence of its mother is distilled through food. The mother's personality comes to fruition in the meals she prepares. Food is a statement of her love, her power and her giving in the family. Food personifies the mother and she is rejected or accepted through it. In this way food, divorced from its biological meaning, takes on a prism of reified projections.

It is well to remember that the mother's centrality to the kitchen during the period since the Second World War occurs under conditions of tension and some coercion. For at the same time that advances in food technology were actually reducing the amount of time a person might need to spend preparing food, women have been simultaneously counseled to spend more time in the kitchen and at the shops, pouring themselves into the food that they present to their families—food that would be the expression of their love and caring. Families gather together around the table twice a day, at breakfast and at dinner. The meals prepared by the mother often became—especially as the children grew and needed her physically less and less—the manifestation of her work for the family, almost a *raison d'être* for her existence. Meals became a chance for the mother to express her originality and her skill while balancing the budget. Due to the limits being set on women's activity and the force of the ideological role of the good mother, those aspects of women's work in the home came to take on enormous meaning and significance. Mealtimes and food became the conveyer belt for all manner of feelings expressed between family members. If giving food was an expression of love on a mother's part, then a child's or husband's positive receptivity to that food became very important. If a woman's self-worth was to be derived in part from her knowledge that she was a good cook, then her self-worth must depend in part on her family's appreciation of her productions. Food is thus always a dynamic in social relationships. The accepting of food makes demands on the receiver. It is about the content and nuances of that relationship.

Just as the baby's experimentation with food can be both exciting and alarming to a mother, so the reworking of

ways of relating that are expressed through food can alarm
and excite the mother of an older child.

There is rarely a child who does not go through food
phases or have strong preferences and dislikes. The spa-
ghetti so relished yesterday and the day before is suddenly
rejected for weeks. Now there has to be baked beans every
suppertime until that palls. The more mushed up the foods
become on the plate, the more interesting to the child
(hence the hamburger replete with extras—the quintessential sweet, savory, hard, soft, chewy food). A plate loaded
with food is required at one time, an almost bare one at
another. The intensity that attaches to these shifts is a stark
reminder of the developmental and interactional issues that
are inseparable from the feeding ambience. (The learning
of table manners, something we all take for granted, is an
aspect of socialization bearing the nuances of class, of
discipline, of what is considered correct and genteel.) Such
issues continue to unfold in the course of development. As
children grow and begin to eat more similarly to their
parents, their idiosyncratic desires may be more or less
accommodated by the parents.

Many parents are able to be relaxed about a child's
attitude towards food, but in thousands and thousands of
families, mealtimes and the taking in or refusal of food
become occasions for discipline and power struggles, sometimes between mother and child, and sometimes between
father and child. Children become aware of the danger of
refusing food. A desire not to eat something may become
translated into a feeling that they are damaging their mother.
They sense themselves hurting/rejecting their mother. In
other words, an initiation may become rephrased as an
attack or a rejection. The mother's desire is internalized by
the child, and the child feels thwarted and confused. The
social role of the mother and the psychology that inevita-

bly follows the taking up of that role are exquisitely expressed in the feeding relationship.

The burden family members may feel about the imperative to appreciate and show enjoyment of the mother's food is best understood not as a pathological need of the mother *per se*, but as a consequence of the limited scope traditionally associated with her social role. We need to keep in mind how the strictures of that role mean that an integral aspect of a woman's self-worth rests on her estimation of herself as a provider of good and nourishing meals. Not surprisingly, the very same pressure family members may be aware of in relating to mother's cooking, is felt by the mother herself in other settings. She may feel obliged to eat and enjoy her own mother's food, or she may identify with the work another woman puts into cooking when she is invited out to dinner. She may feel the need to eat with gusto to show her pleasure at the efforts of her hostess.

In recent years, the trend towards food as a fashion or style has added an extra dimension to the demand that women provide well in the food area. Being an adequate cook is no longer sufficient. Both to vary the routine of daily cooking and because of the incipient pressure to produce imaginative meals, many women spend hours and hours reading cook books, trying new recipes, taking courses in one cuisine or another. Much of this kind of labor is an expression of creativity, for cooking, like other forms of human expression, is also an art. But there is an aspect of this stylized cuisine that focuses on the result and hides the labor process that is embodied in the production of meals. Roz Coward[1] has suggested the similarities that exist between pornography for men and the pictures of the set table replete with gorgeous-looking dishes that are meant to appeal to women. The process of decision-making, shopping, chopping, mixing, cooking and assembling the various ingredients that make up a dish is disguised in the frozen image of fettuccine with walnuts and goat cheese tastefully displayed on the pages of any number of magazines. The ads showing immaculate kitchens with a little girl at the counter drinking her milk and eating her sandwich while her mother looks contentedly on, belie the social process that has taken place to make that interaction possible. The table set for an intimate dinner party of eight with the appetizers surrounding a magnificent centerpiece has the effect of transforming food into the object of status. The food is akin to other objects of adornment such as clothes or jewelry or art, but perhaps it fits the age we live in more appropriately, for it is a perfect example of an object of only momentary value and therefore one which must constantly be replenished.

This stylizing of food is not in itself a new phenomenon, but like many of the phenomena that I am discussing in relation to anorexia and eating problems in general, the take-up of food as fashion is new at a mass cultural level. The *haute bourgeoisie* or aristocracy have always used food as a medium of expression and consolidation of style or as a statement of their times and allegiance. The Russian court adopted a version of French *haute cuisine,* the French Revolution of 1789 itself heralded in a whole new style of cooking. The Chinese imperial court, like many others, refined flavors into a veritable *mélange* of sensual delight. These court-instituted fashions became mandatory practice on the part of those in the *haute bourgeoisie* or the aristocracy who wished to be accepted and become a part of the social life of the ruling class. These highly refined cuisines were made possible by the labor of vast kitchen and kitchen garden staff. The staff itself was highly stratified with chefs and sous-chefs, pastry chefs, sauce chefs and apprentices of all kinds. The results from such kitchens, with their three different stock pots always on the go, are clearly different from what can be reasonably attempted in today's home kitchen, and yet the latter part of the twentieth century has seen the adoption of these styles of cuisine in vast sections of middle-class life in the Western world. This cuisine mimics without modifying the glories of French bourgeois cookery, despite the fact that the contemporary middle-class home kitchen contains but one worker—the wife and mother. It is only very recently that the relative simplicity of *nouvelle cuisine* has seriously challenged the hegemony of French bourgeois cookery as brought to the United States by Julia Child.[2]

The middle-class couple planning a dinner party is still inclined to think in terms of complex sauces requiring discernible layers of stock, roux and wine reductions. Such a meal makes a statement about the importance of the company and the flair of the wife, and, while tasting exquisite and rich, should preferably seem effortless. The work the wife does in preparing such a meal is not seen as work *per se* but as an expression of her giving, her creativity and talent. In the middle echelons of corporate America and Europe throughout the 1950s and 1960s, the importance of the wife as skilled hostess was tacitly recognized in the phenomenon of inviting the boss home to dinner. Before the expense account economy put an end to corporate home entertainment in favor of restaurant meals (with ever more elaborate or, more recently, *nouvelle* menus) a man couldn't go very far in his job, or so the mythology ran, unless his wife could prepare, without appearing to be flustered, an elegant meal for the boss. Succeeding at making dinner for a superior was seen as a prelude to the home entertaining that would be required on the job when visiting businessmen came to town, or as an act of hospitality to peers within the same company or field of business. Thus the wife's labor was a necessary and disguised aspect of the corporate labor process.

This panoply of skills required by the contemporary woman—from the feeding of infants to taking care of the daily food needs of family members, to the role of the hostess with flair—would be interesting enough comment in itself. It suggests that an understanding of women's eating problems must in some sense relate to the complex social role women play as regards food in all of our lives from infancy through adulthood. But before we draw the analysis there, two further issues need to be discussed that shed light on the particulars of eating problems—anorexia, bulimia and compulsive eating as the psychological symptoms of women who are the products of late twentieth-century capitalism.

The first of these points relates to the process of socialization discussed earlier in which mothers are charged with the responsibility for bringing their daughters up to adopt a version of the same social role that they have lived. The process of psychological identification and internalization of the mother's personality (see Chapter 2), which is central in the construction of the daughter's personality, is always imbued with the impact of the social structure. In other words, there is no such thing as a personality constructed outside culture or without reference to its mores, whether these are purposely adopted or consciously disdained. In becoming a girl, one is learning about the ways girls and women are in the world, the centrality of food preparation in their lives, the meanings associated with food as a medium of expression.

A girl grows up with an array of images associated with women and food from her first memories of being fed, to her mother preparing the family meal, to seeing women out shopping, carrying food home, to the images on television and in magazines which frequently locate women in the kitchen. As a result, most girls grow up with a wish to acquire this most central of female attributes, certainly not to the exclusion of developing other aspects of self, but as part of being female. Like periods, dressing, makeup and so on, knowing or anticipating knowing how to cook and hence feed others is just part of the paraphernalia of femininity which girls accept as important to them. Those girls who object to knowing such skills are making a protest within a social context. In other words, their desire to be "unlike women" in these ways is a rejection of aspects of the culture, it is not simply a free choice or even an easy one. The overwhelming cultural pressure to conform makes it extremely hard for individuals to feel comfortable within themselves if they do not take up aspects of their social role deemed so entirely necessary.

It could be objected that not all mothers cook and put the kind of effort into food shopping and preparation that I have described above, and thus do not present their daughters with an image of femininity that is irrevocably linked with food. They do not visit on their daughters a monolithic picture of womanhood in the kitchen, and hence the daughter's heritage does not include the imperative to take up this aspect of her mother's role. While this is increasingly so, especially with working mothers now, the case can be made with no diminishing of persuasion for the mothers who were parenting immediately following the Second World War.

It is only in the last decade or so that not cooking and preparing food for the family has begun to be an option, and many women still feel uneasy about relinquishing that aspect of their social role. The women who were mothering the children who are now anorectic could not exercise that option with any degree of support in the 1950s or 1960s. Even in those cases where there was a supportive husband—one who was happy about defying the stereotyped behavior required of husbands and wives—that family was still set in a cultural context in which not only the neighbors and the women on television did all that was necessary in the kitchen, but also the aunts and grandmothers, and the friends of the mother. A mother, then, would be at odds with what was the norm, and a growing girl had to cope with this knowledge as she was forming her own self by juggling the various images of femininity presented to her. More likely than not, women of the post-Second World War period who were unhappy with their roles as feeders of others, were isolated in their unhappiness. For many women, shame about not wishing to cook accompanies resentment at having to do so. Abdication from a culturally agreed imperative is never done without cost even where open defiance bolsters the person's action. The range of responses that girls and women have to the strictures of their social role, and in particular to those aspects which pertain to the feeding and nurturing of others, are frequently made manifest in the very language of that social role; i.e. in reactions to food and in the development of eating problems.

But the second point that must bear consideration in an analysis of why increasing numbers of young women and women are taking up an anorectic stance relates to a most cruel and ironic aspect of women's relationship to food. So disturbing is this aspect that it is generally glossed over or rather split off, as though what I am about to discuss has nothing to do with those features of women's social role just detailed. Consider for the moment the following shocking fact: a woman comes to know that the food she prepares for others as an act of love and an expression of her caring, is somehow dangerous to the woman herself. Every day women read in any newspaper or magazine of how they must restrain their desire for this very same food. Throughout history women have occupied this dual role of feeding others while needing to deny themselves. But in earlier times, and in many cultures still today, the denial of food, while undoubtedly reflective of the patriarchal social relations, had a rationality based on the economic organization of societies in which food was frequently scarce. The notion took root that the males in the family (first as the hunter, then as the wage-earning breadwinner) should eat before others and consume the most choice morsels. This was to ensure that they received adequate nutrition to enable them to fulfill their economically protective task. The mother would eat after other family members, or she would select a smaller and less desirable portion for herself. Thus the contemporary demand that women restrain themselves in the area of food has echoes with women's role in history. Today, however, the demand is at the level of rhetoric.

Women must hold back their desires for the cakes they bake for others and satisfy themselves with a brine-canned tuna salad with dietetic trimmings. Diet, deprive, deny is the message women receive, or—even more sinister—they must pretend that cottage cheese and melon is as pleasurable as a grilled cheese sandwich for lunch. For a woman, then, food is an object of an entirely different character. It is a potential enemy and a threat. A cardinal rule of femininity, from young women in their teens through women in their fifties, is that they should be desirable. Desirability is linked with an ever-diminishing body size, which is attainable by most women only through severe restrictions on their food intake. And because the "right size" for women has been decreasing yearly since 1965, so women have been encouraged to decrease their food intake yearly.

Fashion in medicine follows wider cultural trends, and the weight tables and correct weights are pared down just as surely as the mannequins who display this year's clothes. Even with new evidence to the contrary that "underweight" is a more serious health risk than marginally "overweight,"[3] particularly a stable overweight, doctors prescribe weight reduction schemes for their patients as though these were a health advantage, without realizing how much their views on current weights reflect current aesthetic ideals. The number of diet books on the best-seller list and the actual numbers of books on dieting sold annually attest to the culture's obsession with restriction of food intake. While these books are increasingly directed to both sexes, the main impetus for the diet books and the main purchasers remain women. Every woman's magazine, from *Vogue* to *Cosmopolitan* to *Family Circle*, carries not only a diet column but a weekly or monthly feature on how to lose weight, or how to stabilize at a lower weight, how to manage food temptations, how to avoid eating "bad" foods.

Almost every woman has had some experience of dieting. Watching what she eats becomes second nature, just a part of being a woman. Women make many different adaptations to the strictures against eating. There are those women who are constantly dieting and consistently limiting their food intakes; there are those women who diet during the week and "let themselves go" at weekends; there are those women who don't eat until suppertime; there are those women who substitute liquid protein for meals several times a week; there are those women who fast once a week; there are those women who haven't eaten potatoes, butter or dessert in years; there are those women who go to the health clubs to work off their "indulgences"; there are those women who binge and then vomit (bulimics); there are those women who consistently plan to diet but end up overeating every time they start to eat something (compulsive eaters); and those women who try to avoid food at all costs (anorectics). The adaptations are endless and women vary their own responses. One week a woman may initiate a frantic exercise programe, the next a plan to restrict food intake, a third week she may "blow it," and so on. Nearly all such adaptations are accompanied by two feelings: shame when those foods which have been deemed forbidden are eaten, and temporary exhilaration when a new plan to control one's desire for the food is envisioned and initiated (for however short a period).

Food for literally millions of women—and here I wish to stress that, horrifying as it is to confront this reality, I do mean millions of women—is a combat zone, a source of incredible tension, the object of the most fevered desire, the engenderer of tremendous fear, and the recipient of a medley of projections centering round notions of good and bad. In the midst of the most extraordinary plenitude the Western world has ever witnessed in regard to food, women in North America, England and Europe are engaged in a battle voluntarily to restrict their food intake, frequently to a point below the actual requirements of their bodies' physiological needs. Whereas fifty years ago women's anxieties were frequently focused around how to get *enough* food for their families and then themselves, today women's anxieties revolve around limiting one's food intake. In restaurants, particularly those that are currently fashionable, we can increasingly witness the spectacle of women picking at the food on their plates as though they weren't really interested, while being able to talk with intensity about the ingredients and the way in which a dish might have been put together. The present style is to favor personal nonchalance as far as one's own food intake is concerned, and yet be in the know about current trends in food fashion. Three exquisitely prepared scallops pass as a main course, one perfectly wrought chocolate truffle as dessert. The cult of asceticism is a most curious handmaiden to the development of food as high style. Eating like a bird is considered feminine and appropriate and almost sanctified. Being able to withstand the temptation to indulge not only earns the admiration and envy of others, it increases one's own feelings of self-esteem. One has resisted where Eve didn't. One has refused the apple.

But just as surely as denial is enviable, so its opposite "indulgence" is comprehensible to all. To fall off the ladder of denial is to enter into cozy communication with others who have suffered similarly. So that if a woman has succumbed out of a lack of vigilance, she surely tells her dinner companions and the conversation predictably shifts not to the food *per se* but to the latest dietary scheme to be pursued. The conversation at many meals is about the food that shouldn't be eaten, the foods that are desired but refused, the weight that must be lost. The appearance of the dessert menu at the restaurant heralds in excitement and trepidation—"Will I be able to resist?", "Maybe I can have it just this once," "Won't someone share (i.e. take responsibility for eating) this with me?" Since women must not eat they know not how to eat or what they wish to eat. They live in the shadow of Eve.[4] They have all sinned.

In *Fat is a Feminist Issue,* I proposed a way of understanding how women's eating problems, those manifest in the activity of compulsive eating, can be understood as a response to this idea that women should not be eating. I discussed how compulsive eating and fat are a protest against the way in which women are regarded in our society as objects of adornment and pleasure. I detailed women's experiences with food and their refusal to conform to the stereotyped images of femininity both in regard to eating and to size. We saw how for many women the eating of large quantities of food gave them, albeit only temporarily, feelings of strength and substance, a kind of stoking up of the emotional furnace so depended upon by others. We saw how fat was often an act of assertion, an attempt to articulate a different femininity, a demand to see the woman not as she is, but as she is fantasized. We saw that fat connotes an uneasily categorizable presence and one that demands active engagement, rather than projection. Fat, I concluded, is an individual (conscious or unconscious) rebellion against an imprisoning social role.

In anorexia nervosa we see yet another form of Eve's defiance, although one that may not perhaps be so immediately apparent. Eve refuses the apple and the knowledge of the world that goes with it in a gesture that can be understood as a rejection of that world and of that knowledge. While at first glance it might appear that the anorectic's refusal to eat is an act of conformity, a taking-up of the commandment, the act of refusal contains its dialectical response: I shall not partake of that which is offered for it is not sufficient/not for me at all. The food is the symbolic representation of a world that has already disappointed the anorectic. Entry into it is not the answer.

For the compulsive eater the experience of eating, while fraught with anxiety, contains elements of soothing, and the impulse towards food is generally coupled with a desire to give to oneself, to quiet an upset, to make whole what is empty, to say what cannot be spoken. The anorectic can find no such momentary satisfaction in the taking-in of that most basic substance of life. Whether or not food was ever experienced by the anorectic as soothing and life-giving we can only speculate, for we cannot know how the early feeding ambience was experienced by her as a baby. We have the sense that for the compulsive eater, the early feeding relationship was a source of pleasure and relief for the person, that food was presented to provide comfort and engendered feelings of safety. Although in the process the hunger mechanism may well have been tampered with, producing in its wake all sorts of problems for the child and later the adult vis-à-vis food, the important point to be made in this context is that food was essentially

a positive experience. However, the extent of fearful feelings that food arouses in women who come to be anorectic
suggests that early eating experiences were themselves tense
and problematic; that the feeding relationship was invested
with anxiety.

Many anorectic women, in talking of mealtimes at home,
mention being party to one of two completely contradictory features that they were aware of as children in relation
to food: rigid order or chaotic confusion. In Jean's house
meals were served with a punctuality more usually found
on the shop floor. As though a whistle were being blown, it
was crucial that all family members appear in concert for
breakfast, supper and lunch at weekends. Grace would be
said, and in an atmosphere of solemnity the gift of food
would be ingested by all, each family member being required to eat all that was on his or her plate. Conversation
was limited to non-controversial topics that would not
upset Mother. This meant that academic work and politics
could not be discussed. Family occasions, Grandma, Father's job arrangements and so on were the most usual
subjects of conversation. The atmosphere was tense and
joyless. Food was not something to be enjoyed or "indulged" in. Second helpings were frowned on, dessert was
always less exciting than the children desired. No one was
permitted to miss a meal without adequate notice. A calen-
dar hanging in the kitchen detailed the week's coming
menu and, exceptional circumstances apart, several days'
notice was considered polite if a meal was to be missed.

The rigidity surrounding food extended to other aspects
of Jean's home life. Getting-up and going-to-bed times
were strictly regulated, as were times for homework, playing
in the garden and watching TV. The grown-ups had no
more flexibility than they allowed their children. Home
life was a series of jobs to be performed as designated by
the parents. There was at the same time little privacy and

little engagement. Each person was expected to perform the task of being a human being in a self-contained way within the structure.

Lisa's family expressed the other pole. Mealtimes were chaotic. Sometimes there was what approximated to a conventional-looking meal for all, sometimes each person ate something different. The family never quite managed to sit down together or sustain a whole mealtime without interruptions. The phone was always ringing, the children fought, people left the table as soon as they felt like it, friends were always welcome and the conversation did not appear to hold any restrictions, making it seem random and unconnected. An atmosphere was thus created which belied the intense enmeshment of family members. Lisa's father and mother were both overweight.

Curiously, while the mother's input into both these types of dinner table was certainly distinct, the time spent in food preparation was not noticeably different. In both households the mother put a lot of effort into what ultimately arrived at the table. In the second of the two households described, the food preferences of the family members were noted and attended to, while in the first, the mother's energy went into the planning of nutritional and economical meals. The mother's presence at mealtimes was as strongly felt as it had been in earlier life.

In both Lisa's and Jean's cases, the anorectic response encapsulated both the desire to be like and the need to be different from the family. Jean's anorexia took a fairly conventional course (and in looking back one can almost predict its onset). It started early, when she was eleven, shortly after the appearance of her first menstrual period, an event that greatly distressed her mother. Her mother expressed a horror that her period should arrive so inopportunely, and Jean took this to mean that she had done something terribly wrong. Something in her development

was out of sequence and it must be her fault. By reducing
her food intake below the weight at which she would
menstruate, she saw to it that she never got her period
again.

Jean elevated the rigidity of family meals to an extreme,
allowing herself only a certain number of mouthfuls per
meal of any given foodstuff and a certain number of bites
per mouthful. She ceased eating after 6 p.m. (after reading
in a magazine that the food did not get digested as speedily
after that hour); she rationed the time she allowed herself
to watch the television sitting down; she instituted an
exercise programe; she meticulously planned the time to
spend on homework, and so on. She did all these things in
an attempt to achieve a certain (self-) acceptance that was
lacking. She felt that if she could only apply and follow
the family code better than anyone else, then she could
garner some respect and hence self-esteem.

Jean made a point of getting up earlier than anyone else
in the family, of keeping her room tidier than all the
others, of requiring less food than anyone else. Her main
efforts focused around food. She was incorporating the
regimented family way of doing things while simultaneously
rejecting the most obvious symbol of family togetherness.
For as her meals got progressively smaller, she found it
extremely difficult to be at the breakfast and dinner table,
and would cause the most enormous upset to the family
system by her actions. She was rejecting what the family
had to offer while at the same time making her protest in a
way that reflected family form. In her anorexia she was
attempting to be both like and unlike the family. She was
engaged in a process where she was attempting to disen-
gage, and yet because she had been emotionally under-
nourished throughout her childhood, she was still in great
need of succor. A differentiated self was thus impossible,
she could only mimic what she had absorbed as a way of

providing herself with some protection in the attempted separation.

In later chapters we will look more closely at the underlying psychodynamics of the family, and Jean's resulting psychology. For the present, I want to draw the parallels that existed in the family feeding situation and Jean's uptake of the symptom. But as I do this I am aware of the time in which Jean reached adolescence (1971) and the cultural preoccupation with thinness and food management that prevailed then. For I am quite convinced that the psychopathology she exhibited, although expressed in anorexia, could well have been expressed in a different form if she had grown up at a different time. Thirty years ago the very same environment at home creating a similar psychology might have found a solution not in anorexia but in a cluster of obsessive symptoms. (Such symptoms might have bound up the anxiety she experienced as effectively as did the anorexia.) She might well have instituted a series of rituals, not related to diet or weight but to washing or counting or locking doors and so on—acts that in themselves would have been as understandable and psychologically opaque as the anorexic stance.

Thirty years ago, a young woman would not necessarily have sought a solution to low self-esteem through the transformation of her body and the drastic denial of a biological aspect of her femininity. For she would not have grown up in a culture preoccupied by the abundance of food linked with a need for girls and women to deprive themselves of it. The asceticism practiced in her own home would have been less at odds with the confusing edicts of the culture in general. Food, not yet a consumer commodity, would not have been imbued with its current significance. Body-image, while important, was not the beginning and end of experience for women. Anorexia would have been a much less appropriate response and protest. It would have been rather more unfathomable, and given that psychological symptoms express the ideas a culture has at any given time about itself, a different protest would have emerged.

Lisa's anorexia developed fairly late in life at the age of twenty-six. Throughout her adolescence and years of young adulthood she was plagued with compulsive eating and a seesawing up and down the scales in the never-ending search for a solution to get slim. Like Jean's, her anorexia also represented a premature attempt at separation from the family—not premature in years in the way Jean's was, but in that there were many things Lisa still perceived she needed from the family and could not do without emotionally. Her fat and her compulsive eating had represented an attempt both to be like her parents and to create a shield between her and them. She felt herself to be chaotic inside and "a mess." When she lost weight she could deny this unruly, messy part of herself but it did not stay repressed or split off for long and eventually she would break out of her diet and the cycle would restart. In her mid-twenties she married John, an accountant, a man whose job and personality contained just what Lisa felt to be lacking in hers. He was methodical and orderly. Determined and patient, he could tolerate what Lisa found excruciating. She found him soothing and reassuring and she felt temporarily safe. Her eating behavior became much less chaotic and she stabilized at a weight that felt comfortable to her. After several years the marriage dissolved. They had become locked into the roles they played for each other, John providing the structure, Lisa providing the emotion and sociability for him. The breakup left Lisa without much-needed boundaries in which her "free" part could roam. Although she had initiated the breakup, the effects of it left her devastated. She felt guilt and insecurity at the same time. She began to believe that she was the rejected one and she felt herself flailing about. She was nervous about being single and in the position of looking for a partner. She couldn't bear to feel so exposed and vulnerable.

As she began to scrutinize what was wrong with her, she decided it was her body, and that she would be more acceptable and appear less needy if she could resemble the untouchable ladies stalking the pages of *Vogue*. She got slimmer and slimmer and, having a large frame, she looked longer and longer and increasingly remote and untouchable. She developed disdain for food and those who ate, including the part of her that expressed such a basic need. Food and eating, previously experienced as soothing and potentially pleasurable, turned into dangerous, contemptible activities. Because she was really very hungry and used to relating to food in a positive way, she had to work hard to repress her impulses towards food. To this end, she developed a series of rituals, such as only eating one egg a day divided into four sections, each of which had to be eaten with a minimum space of four hours between them. She allowed herself a daily tube of peppermints—a maximum of one to be sucked hourly. She prepared a huge undressed salad for the evening, extending the process of preparation for as long as possible by chopping all the ingredients into different shapes and then eking out the time she would take to eat it. Her ideal was to eat only half of what she prepared, and this over the course of half an hour; the other half she would take to bed to eat while she watched television. In addition, she would buy a small carton of yoghurt and a muffin daily. She would restrict herself to eating a third of the carton of yoghurt and half the muffin—the rest she threw away. These rituals had a dual effect. On the one hand they reassured her that she could keep away from food and on the other hand they provided a version of the structure she had so needed her husband for. The anorexia became a way to bind her worries and anxieties, to create boundaries (albeit false boundaries) and to seek relief and security in an outwardly acceptable self-image. Her family's food habits began to repulse her viscerally and she wished to be as different from them as possible. Ritualistic food deprivation became a solution to a complex of intrapsychic problems.

Again, I wish to stress that the particular configuration of Lisa's psyche, while it predisposed her to develop a psychological symptom which could bind the feelings of messiness and chaos inside, would not in a different historical period have led so directly to taking up anorexia nervosa. Her psychology would have much in common with the cases in the literature of pre-orgasmic or ''frigid'' women found two or three decades ago. Typically, such women were unable to experience sexual pleasure personally, but in an attempt to get satisfaction they were for the norm of their day often considered promiscuous or nymphomaniacs. The frigidity expressed, like the anorexia, a withdrawn attitude, involuntary closedness, and inability to open up and let go psychologically and physically. The fear, when analyzed, was that the letting down of the false boundaries that frigidity symbolized, would lead to feelings of disintegration; the chaos that lived locked up inside would gush forth, rendering the woman vulnerable and shattering her to (psychic) pieces. The involuntary frigidity (which could be more or less extreme ranging from inorgasmic to vaginisimic) was the somatized solution such a psychic structure sought as a means of defense. For today's women, where the sexual taboos are considered, though they may not be a thing of the past, the test of acceptance is deemed to come through the attainment of a perfect body-image. The attempt both to achieve this and yet reject it at the same time situates psychological difficulties in the more visible aspects of the body.

How and why the body has become for women the

vehicle for self-expression is the subject of the next chapter. I ask the reader to keep in mind from this chapter the overwhelming power of food in women's lives, the role of women as feeders of others and curtailers of food for themselves. For without this structural relationship to food, the ability of our culture to breed body insecurity in women would be seriously impaired.

## NOTES

1. Coward, R., *Female Desire* (London, 1984).
2. Beck, S., Bertholle, L. and Child, J., *Mastering the Art of French Cooking* (New York, 1961).
3. Sorlie P., Gordon, T. and Kannel, W., "Body Build and Mortality, the Framingham Study," *Journal of the American Medical Association*, 243 (1980), 1828–31.
4. My thanks to Janet Surrey for pointing out to me that it was Eve's eating of the apple that brought us out of a state of grace.

# 4  The Breeding of
Body Insecurity

The receptivity that women show to body insecurity is set
against a background of contradictory images and meanings assigned to women's bodies in general. Precisely
because of the vicissitudes of social overlay, the development of a personal and stable body-image is extremely
problematic for women. How women see and experience
their bodies refers to cultural factors outside themselves. In
addition, the individual woman can feel a pronounced
variation during the course of an hour, a day or a week
towards her body. How she feels about her body will
frequently affect how she is feeling about herself at that
particular moment. How she feels within herself influences
how she feels about her body. A felt acceptability in one
area tends to extend to the other, so that being in a "good
mood" may predispose her to find her body acceptable,
even pleasing. For many women the immediate feeling of
a sense of self is inextricable from momentary feelings
about their bodies. The body is perceived as acceptable or
unacceptable, providing a foundation for self-concept. At
one moment a woman may experience herself as large and
ungainly, at another as slim and attractive. Her body shape
and size do not actually have to change for her body to

receive such projections. The ideas she has about herself that she sees in her body are sufficiently powerful to influence what she expresses physically.[1] If she feels comfortable in herself she carries herself in one way, if she feels a dis-ease it is expressed in another.

Throughout Western history, from the art and mythology of ancient civilization to current representational forms, women's bodies have been regarded as objects of beauty as well as symbols of what constitutes beauty. A beautiful woman confers additional status on a man by implying his command over it. With or through her body, a woman makes her way in the world. In much the same way as a man's sense of well-being rests on his knowledge of himself as a provider (at whatever level that may be), so a woman's identity is deeply entwined with a sense of herself as an attractive person and with a body with which she negotiates the world. The commoditization of sexuality discussed earlier reaches its apex in the way in which women are schooled to relate to their bodies as their objects/tools/weapons in the marketplace of social relations. In addition, as we shall see, a woman's body is a feared and wanted object for both women and men. Into this discordant tapestry of meaning, of bodies for nurturance, bodies for satisfaction and bodies for sale, each woman has to find a way to live in and with her body from a position that does not predispose her to feel a great deal of comfort or ease. Thus the body-image she fashions and projects for herself is forged under extremely difficult circumstances and not surprisingly often feels precarious.

Awaiting this precariously constructed self-image lies the mammoth power of the diet/fashion/cosmetic/beauty industries. These industries have both material and ideological thrusts. Their commercial exigencies are the motivating force for their existence, and their profits are sustained on the enormity of the body insecurity that they both identify and allege to ameliorate while simultaneously reinforcing and amplifying this very insecurity.

At various stages in history and in different societies, women have striven to make their bodies conform to the local culture's idea of what constitutes sexual attractiveness. Since the Renaissance, the ideal has swung between an emphasis on buxomness and its opposite, the Victorian eighteen-inch waist. In nineteenth-century America, the first sixty years are marked by a preference for the "frail, pale, willowy woman."[2] In 1865 the English music hall-style beauty swept the American imagination in the form of Lillian Russell, and the "voluptuous woman" was all the rage. Towards the end of the century the tall, athletic Gibson girl was in vogue, giving way in the 1910s to its diminutive extension, the small, boyish model as exemplified by Mary Pickford and Clara Bow. The flat-chested flapper reigned during the 1920s, but from the 1930s through to the end of the 1950s, feminine beauty was again represented by voluptuousness and curves, big breasts and nipped-in waists. While deviations were always tolerated, and indeed oppositional currents or more than one current were running at one time, the dominant images extended over epochs.

A striking feature of the last twenty-five years has been the acceleration in the rate of change in what are considered desirable body types for women. As though they were hemlines that could be shortened or lengthened seasonally, the current aesthetic of women's bodies has been changing almost yearly. Since the 1960s women's bodies—as reflected in fashion magazines, glamorous serials on television and the media in all its forms—have been getting slimmer and slimmer and slimmer. Gone are the bosoms of the 1950s; spiraling angularity is *à la mode* today. Whereas fifty years ago many women might bemoan the fact that their bodies did not conform to the reigning ideal, *no* woman today can rest assured in the knowledge that she has a good figure. For no woman today has the right body for more than a season or two. The aesthetic ideal is ever changing.

It is not simply that the last few decades have witnessed an acceleration in the rate of changing aesthetics of the female form, but that this has coincided with the rise of interest in fashion and body-image among the majority of women. Until this century, these changes in body desirability were of principal concern to women of the haute bourgeoisie, courtesans and certain sections of the bourgeoisie. The advent of the department store, the woman's magazine, the participation in mass culture and, in America especially, the process of assimilation of immigrants from pre-industrial cultures, are factors that have coalesced to create an enormous pressure on women to identify their interests with the clothes and bodies of the mannequins and movie stars. High fashion is reproduced at every economic level. Indeed, in the United States department stores democratically sell and display the same cut of clothes in different price ranges on different floors. From the bargain basement to the designer salon, individualized boutiques cater to the different purses of women shoppers. The impact of movies, television and mass culture in general has created a population responsive to imitate and take up the received images of femininity. These images project a few limited body types for women, and the designated female beauties of the moment correspond to these body types. Because we live in an age in which thinness has been seen to be increasingly desirable, and because thinness is a stated aim of the anorectic, the question ''why thinness?'' and what it represents in the last twenty-five years, bears some looking at.

Slimness as femininity (and then moral value) appeared first in the early 1960s. Jean Shrimpton, ''the Shrimp,'' the

upper-middle-class English woman, was the first mannequin goddess of the time who broke distinctly with the
voluptuous images of women exemplified by Marilyn Mon-
roe, Gina Lollobrigida, Jayne Mansfield and Brigitte Bar-
dot. Shrimpton's slim, long-legged, small-breasted body
and free-flowing straight hair represented a rejection of
the rigidity of English class society. (Julie Christie became
her counterpart in the movies.) That she was from the
upper middle class was perhaps no accident. The original
1960s' trendsetters of the fashion in body style and clothes
came out of the ranks of the upper-middle and upper class.
The very thing they exemplified was an individualistic
break with the constraints of class society that only the
privileged could express. Promoted by magazines representing that class—*Vogue, Queen, Harper's,* etc.—Jean
Shrimpton was shown wearing the clothes of Mary Quant,
Ossie Clark and other upper-middle-class designers breaking free from the stuffiness of the 1950s by proclaiming a
new womanhood that was single, sexy, adventurous and
free.

This freedom was further expressed by the exploits of
the Jet Set, the sons and daughters of the old aristocracy in
England and the new in America, who flaunted convention
openly and determined to live a wild life gobbling up new
sensations in art, music, dance and clothes, thus spawning
a style that broke radically with the conventions and mores
of the 1950s. The Jet Set were uniformly thin. Whether
this was because they just happened to be long-legged,
horsey ectomorphs, as was often said at the time, or
whether there was a prize in thinness *per se* as a rejection
of the display of the fat of wealth, it isn't possible to
judge. Suffice it to say that thinness signified a freedom,
one which increasing numbers of people from all class
backgrounds could take up. It was a break with the past
and seemed to offer the possibility of transcendence of

class itself. This latter thrust became more apparent in the emergence and popularity of kitchen sink drama, British playwrights of the 1960s grappling with reality and class—Kops, Wesker, Pinter, Arden, Dunn; the music of the Beatles, a working-class group from the north of England; and in the person of Twiggy, perhaps the most famous model of the decade, born Lesley Huggins and hailing from the working-class community of Dagenham. Twiggy was very slim and quite small. She didn't hide her working-class background and for millions of young women in Britain especially, she carried the jet-setters' message of freedom and a good time through to the working and middle classes.[3]

In 1960s' America there was not so much a response to class relations *per se,* as a challenge to the sexual and racial stratification that existed in every sphere of life. There was a challenge to government policies at every level including military decisions, and the youth of America were instrumental in defying the world of their elders. This translated, at its lowest common denominator, as a youth rebellion, and from there it was a short step to the packaging of youth that has become a dominant motif in American life from the late 1960s until the present. The post-Second World War baby boom grew up creating, and receptive to, new consumer markets and youthful energy, and staying young was celebrated. Youth, or rather the struggle against aging, became paired with thinness. Even well-established movie stars reduced their bodies to conform to new, thinner, youthful standards. Anne Bancroft shed her siren image of the late 1950s, Jane Fonda lost the fleshy sexiness of Barbarella, Mary Tyler Moore left behind the role of wife on television and slimmed down for her role as the independent woman. Even Sophia Loren went down a size or two. Thinness seemed to nullify and transcend the exigencies of time as though age and aging were states to be avoided at all costs.

Recently Jane Fonda, stepping down from the pedestal of the movie star image to share her way of staying young and slim, has managed to be honest about the ravaging effects of being bulimic, while marketing a similarly obsessive solution—exercise. America, the great equalizer, now has us all fighting age and flab. The new evangelists preach exercise to stay thin, fit and young. Slimness and fitness have become part of the American dream. In America, thinness bears witness to the attempt to deny human biology and the process of development. As the real youth enter a shrinking job market with fewer and fewer opportunities, the youth of fifteen years ago, as a group with a great deal of surplus income and well-defined consumer interest, strives to go on being young for as long as possible: the advertising agencies and their media handmaidens keep alive the notion of their unstinting vitality which needs to be recharged by the toys that a consumer economy can produce. Should the individual find herself unable to maintain the superficial exuberance of youth, there is always the professional help of the cosmetic surgeon. No longer simply the preserve of the very rich and of movie stars, face and body resculpting doctors offer their wares daily through the pages of New York's two mass circulation dailies, *The New York Post* and *The Daily News*. Tucking and lifting is being done earlier and earlier so that the "new youth" can keep up with its young idea of itself.

For many of the new youth (thirty to forty-five), two other social factors that have affected their lives find perverse expression in thinness. One relates to the impact of feminism and the other to the growing tendency to have smaller families. Looking at feminism first, one is struck by the Women's Liberation Movement's critique of women as sexual objects for men, coinciding with the increasing objectification of parts of women's bodies—lips, legs, hair, breasts, eyebrows and so on—by the fashion and beauty industry in general. As millions of women have sought to change the definition of self based on a physicality that conforms to the stereotypes they are sold, searching instead for new ways to conceive their identity and their place in the world, so there would appear to be a subversive attempt to undermine these changes, for there is a dramatic increase in the number of words written and sold about how women should look and be in their bodies. Confidence at work will be gained by "dressing for success," confidence in bed by the right underwear, lingerie and perfume, confidence in general by being as slim as can be.

In *Fat is a Feminist Issue* I suggested that a smaller body size for women was being proposed just at that moment in history when women were demanding to be taken more seriously in the workplace and, in the language of the 1970s, "demanding more space." The shrinking of the American and British woman, or rather the idea that she should shrink, coincides too uncomfortably with changes women have been demanding about their social role for one to regard it as merely coincidence. Body maintenance, body beautiful, exercise and the pursuit of thinness are offered as valued arenas for concern precisely at the moment when women are trying to break free of such imperatives.

Along with women's increased interest in the workplace as a source of identity and meaning,[4] there has been a decrease in family size and a corresponding increase in the breakup of traditional families in the United States and England. The decrease in family size can be ascribed to many factors, not the least a kind of economic prosperity which has meant a lower mortality rate throughout the

Western world, and the desire of women to make a contribution outside the home. In times when child-bearing was seen as the feminine experience and the only legitimate role for women, the presence of hips or, to put it another way, the full figure associated in the popular mind with child-bearing, was revered. Now, in a gross denial of women's capacity to bear children, hips are disparaged. The message is almost as pernicious as "You can't have it both ways," or "If you are going to, you had better not flaunt it." Hence the implied directive to conceal the physically maternal side of oneself. Slimness is opposed to fertility. In this regard, Twiggy's pre-pubescent thinness sets up the association of the ideal of femininity as being separate from woman as fecund and child-bearing. A pre-pubescent body cannot reproduce. Thus Twiggy's size and cuteness played a supporting role in the contemporary version of women's bodies being made into objects.

And finally there is the role of the fashion industry whose capricious desires come to taunt all women when they confront the clothes in their closets on a daily basis. Just as one feels comfortable in the clothes one has selected, the style changes, and for the last twenty years current fashions have been displayed on extremely slim bodies. It is hard to view the androgynous slant that can be seen in the clothes and bodies staring out from magazines and billboards as sympathetic to women. Indeed, Calvin Klein's most recent underwear ad for women shows an extremely lithe woman in a pair of men's styled jockey shorts. One has to do a double take to assess whether the image being presented is indeed that of a man or a woman.

So thinness as a contemporary ideal symbolizes many different things. To give it its most progressive sense, it can be understood as an attempt to transcend barriers of class and age, while in its more negative sense it is yet another reworked expression of misogynist tendencies alive in the culture, from a denial of the shape of the feminine form to an attack on how much room a woman should occupy. It is offered as a way out of reality and promoted as the entry to, and badge of, the good life.

In order to understand more fully how each individual woman comes to feel from the *inside* that she must respond to the call of the diet/fashion/body beautiful industries, we need to comprehend how body insecurity works at an intra-psychic level. In providing a framework to consider this, I will draw upon clinical and theoretical work in psychoanalysis as it provides us with the fine-grained texture required if we are to understand the steps involved in the acquisition of a corporeal sense of self. As I discuss some of the findings of psychoanalysis I hope the reader can hold on to the tension that exists between the two modes of inquiry—the outside and the inside, the sociological and the psychoanalytic—so that the social roots of the individual's experience are read into the account I am about to give.

The attainment of a corporeal sense of a self is not a sudden event that occurs at a particular stage of development but is better understood as a fundamental aspect of becoming human. Modern psychoanalytic theorists describing developmental processes both from the vantage point of direct child observations[5] and from the reconstruction of infantile mental processes through psychoanalysis, have tried to create a picture of the physical and psychological growth of the neonate up to and through its birth as a human, i.e. social, being. The notion of the self becoming a subject and realizing the physical boundaries of subjectivity is a knotty problem in developmental theory, for that very recognition itself implies a split between the psyche and the soma. Winnicott, in an attempt to argue against such a split, writes: "The live body, with its limits, and with an inside and an outside, is felt by the individual to form the core for the imaginative self."[6] Spitz[7] talks of the existence of two systems, the co-anaesthetic (the bodily) and the diacritic (the emotional). The first of these, the co-anaesthetic, is eventually fused with the diacritic as the latter becomes more highly developed within the context of the infant's relationship with its mother. Mahler, Pines and Bergman[8] surmise that the development of body aware-ness is linked to the process of separation–individuation, starting tentatively at around six months and continuing through until individuation is achieved at twenty-four months. From nine to fourteen months, as the baby devel-ops more motor activity, the mother in turn begins to name the various body parts for the baby. In mirroring the child's interest in its physicality she helps build its sense of body awareness. From fourteen to twenty-four months, Mahler observes the baby being active with its body in relation to its mother; the body becomes a vehicle for differentiation and the baby may resist being put in various positions, such as the reclining one. As psychological separateness is proceeding, so the body becomes the vehi-cle for manifesting more independent activity.

I myself am inclined to take the view which assumes that for the first few months the infant's life is primarily one of sensation. The infant is essentially merged with its primary caretaker (usually the mother) and does not yet have a sense of itself as a separate being at any level. Neither, would I argue, does it make sense to talk of a split between the psyche and the soma, but rather of a unity. It is with the development of complex mental func-tioning that occurs within the context of a relationship that an awareness of an I, which I take to be a physical/mental unit, is recognized as separate but related to others. The person can only recognize its subjectivity in relation to the subjectivity (both physical and mental) of others. In other words, the development of a corporeal sense of self is entirely related to the development of object relations (relations to others beginning with the recognition of the mother as a person, an object separate from oneself), and the distortions that can come to occur in the person's recognition of their own physicality are consequences of difficulties in those object relations.

Psychological and physical development of the infant are dependent on the relationship that develops between it and the person who is looking after it, its caretaker, usually the mother (in psychoanalytic development theory terms, the object). The infant uses the personality, the psyche of the caretaker in its development of its own ego structure. The caring and attention of the mother is the food which nourishes the embryonic psyche of the baby so that it can develop into personhood. In Chapter 1 we saw the impact of gender prescriptions on mothering. We took account of the fact that mothers are bound to have many complex feelings about themselves, about their capacities, their needs, their desires and their feelings about mothering. We saw how raising a daughter called up a particular set of difficult emotions in women because the requirements of successful femininity make special demands in the mother–daughter relationship both at conscious and unconscious levels.

The mother has the job of introducing her daughter to personality characteristics that conform in broad terms with the culture's notion of appropriateness for girls. The mother's identification with a same-sexed infant means that in raising a daughter she is in a profound sense reproducing herself. Most women live with feelings of self-disgust and dislike (hidden or open) because of the process of psychological and social femininity they have lived through. Therefore in relating to a baby girl, a mother is inevitably transmitting some negative feelings about being female. In addition, the acquisition of gender identity—the knowl-

edge of oneself as a girl or as a boy—is learned simultaneously with the stereotypically acceptable behaviors of
that gender. For mothers raising girl children in the period
following the Second World War, the stereotyped views of
femininity were restricting, subordinating and, from
today's perspective, denigrating.

The mother–daughter relationship is shaped by the social world that mothers live in and daughters must enter.
The mother's psychology itself was shaped with reference
to that world by her own mother. In this world two key
features of women's psychology are that women should
not be emotionally dependent, but instead provide a dependent relationship for others, and that they should not initiate and act, but perform the role of midwife to the aspirations
of others. As a result of these underpinnings in feminine
psychology, women come to feel hesitant about their needs,
and indeed their very selves, and they are encouraged to
seek validation by looking to others to award it. A girl
grows up learning to turn much of her attention outside
herself, both to attend to the needs of others and to achieve
the approval of others by mirroring their projections.

Girls gravitate towards the expertise of others and deny,
ignore, or suppress many needs and initiatives that arise
internally. The result is that they grow up with a sense of
never having received quite enough, and often feel insatia-
ble and unfulfilled. As an attempted solution to this psychic state of affairs, they seek connection with others and
learn that this connection, especially with men, depends on
the acceptability of their bodies.

The early mother–child relationship is an essentially
sensual one. The model of relating revolves around hugging, cuddling, feeding, changing, dressing, rocking and
the meeting of "presumed" physical distress. Many mothers enjoy the physical exchange with their infants. As the
child grows, the mother introduces and organizes for the

baby its physical development. She helps it to sit and stand and encourages its attempts to crawl and walk by holding her arms outstretched in a welcoming gesture and applauding its new achievements. At the same time as she relates to the baby's increasing physical accomplishments, she is organizing other stimuli in a psycho-physical unity. The repertoire of actions the baby can take expands vis-à-vis its desires for food and drink, and provided the mother can respond to such initiations, the baby will come to interpret particular physiological cues as hunger and others as signals of satisfaction. It will distinguish between desire for food and desire for drink and so on until, if introduced to a wide variety of tastes and textures, it will be able to discriminate between them and, as it develops the capacity for language, it will be able to match finely discriminated internal desires with the expectation of getting what it wants.

The mother responds to other psycho-physical cues the baby emits. She tries to assess when it is tired and to provide the environment that makes sleep possible; she responds to the baby's body temperature and dresses it to achieve maximum comfort; she checks its nappies so that it does not experience discomfort for too long. In all these ways, the mother and the mother–child relationship is the vehicle for the baby's capacity to understand its physical–psychological world. The baby then develops a corporeal sense of self entwined with its psychological—"the imaginative self" of Winnicott.

Before we leave our discussion of this psyche–soma unity, let us recall the social context that shapes the mother–daughter relationship in such ways that the perhaps idyllic view described of mother and child cooperating rhythmically, is often far from the case. Into the picture I have drawn we need to insert those aspects of sex-role stereotyping and gender-specific prohibitions which impinge on the "free" exploration and satisfaction of the baby's developing initiations. As regards the increased motor activity of the child, we need to bear in mind that while a mother may have little hesitancy about enabling her daughter to crawl and walk, she will at some point temper her enthusiasm for the daughter's growing physical independence because of the social lessons she needs to impart to her. Many will protest that such crude stereotyping hardly exists, but it is a rare mother who does not discourage her daughter from exploring in the woods (in a way she might unthinkingly encourage a son). Girls are discouraged from climbing dangerous-looking trees and ladders: if they are not actively dissuaded, a sense of danger (not one to be overcome and mastered, but one to be avoided) is transmitted to them. Girls are taught to sit properly with their legs crossed, to walk in a ladylike fashion, to exercise restraint in physical matters. They are generally discouraged from exploring their vulvas and vaginas. The development of secondary sexual characteristics in adolescence is often accompanied by mixed feelings about bodily functions, as parents, and especially mothers, have not been able to convey in an unambiguous manner the positive aspects of female sexuality.

In introducing her daughter to her body, a mother has an awareness of the dramatic ways in which a woman's body can change during its lifetime. The development of breasts is the prelude to the physiological changes that occur during a woman's fertility and during pregnancy and lactation. In gross terms, a man's body is a relatively stable affair. A woman's body visibly changes during the course of the menstrual cycle. These changes are part of each woman's experience of herself and what she passes on to her daughter. The way young women are encouraged to be in their bodies—restrained and contained—is strikingly at odds with the actual physical potential that their bodies hold.

At the same time that mothers transmit caution and limitation, where the physical expression of their daughter is concerned, they are consciously and unconsciously monitoring and shaping another important aspect of their daughter's physicality—their appetites. We have seen how critical the mother's role is in introducing us all to food and the feeding ambience; and I have suggested that the feeding relationship is as affected by gender as are other aspects of maternal care. What concerns us here is the impact that femininity (as currently conceived) imposes on the feeding relationship between mother and daughter. Not surprisingly, cultural dictates are reflected in a mother's actions vis-à-vis a daughter's appetites. In general, mothers wean their daughters earlier, and each feeding period is considerably shorter for girl infants than boy infants. Girls are thought to need less food than boys, and it would be hard to say whether this attitude springs from our current cultural aesthetics or from physiological evidence. What it is possible to comment on is the anxiety that mothers (and to a lesser extent fathers and other parental figures) express about whether their daughters are eating enough or eating too much. The mother herself, the recipient of daily messages to restrain her desire for food so that she can be the right size for today, brings a version of that worry to her daughter. She wishes to feed her well and healthily, but at the same time such attempts may be undermined by concerns that the child may turn out "greedy" and want too much. Other mothers, unable to feed themselves appropriately, engage with their daughter's food needs to the point of obsessiveness. Through the process of projective identification, they encourage their daughters to eat whatever they want, thus reaping some narcissistic gratification in the process. Still others, reluctant to loosen the connection that feeding symbolizes, offer the breast or bottle as a means of comfort to a baby when the child is seeking soothing in other forms. The baby's separation from the breast or bottle leaves its mother at a loss, for it is such a central way she had of giving and of shaping the relationship. The mother's actions with a boy child may share similar features, but there is an important distinction. In relating to a boy, she is not struggling to overcome a feeling of identification in herself. He is not the same as her. In addition, the social requirements of masculinity do not command the same kind of restraint on man's desire for food. He does not need to be denied in the first place.

While it might be hard to imagine the subtle transactions that occur around feeding in infancy, they are obvious during adolescence when the young woman's bodily changes precipitate a whole range of reactions around the family dinner table. Mothers are often involved in encouraging daughters to diet for the first time to get rid of "puppy fat" or pimples. Food restraint, previously exercised by the mother, or talked about at least if not acted on, now becomes the domain of the two females who may either cooperate or squabble over it.

The consequences of such influences in the mother–daughter relationship are that the mechanisms of hunger and satisfaction are frequently tampered with so that internal cues which arise in the daughter's body are misinterpreted. She is then left with a confusion about the two elemental physical–psychological states of feeling hungry and feeling satisfied. She may not be able to tell the difference between these two feelings or, if she can, she may not know how to act on them in a straightforwardly satisfying way. This unconscious thwarting of the daughter's hunger and satisfaction mechanism comes to play an important part in later life in a girl's receptivity to looking outside herself for information about food, hunger and satisfaction as well as for a sense of well-being in her body. The misdirecting of these internal physical cues does not aid the development of a secure body-image. Rather, it opens up the possibility that a girl will feel insecure in and with her body and become a target for the hugely profitable enterprises of the diet/fashion/cosmetics/body beautiful industry.

Beyond the implications at the purely physical level, the dictates of the mother–daughter relationship predispose a daughter to seek acceptability and guidance outside herself. A girl is frequently discouraged in both obvious and subtle ways from taking the initiative where desires of her own which might conflict with female sex-role stereotyping are concerned. A girl is applauded for offering to share, for initiating activities which smooth the way for others, for helping. It is commonplace to see a girl interested in science diverted into biological or life sciences or nursing (depending upon her class background). This gross sex-role stereotyping has its equivalent in how girls' early interests and initiatives are managed. One only has to look at a sandpit or swings in the park to see the wild abandon of the boys compared to the general demureness of the girls. Girls who are as unruly as the boys win the appellation "tomboys," thus confirming the cultural notion that tearing around, following one's inner impulses, is essentially a boyish activity. In not being encouraged to develop her initiating part and draw a sense of authenticity and strength from that (including at the physical level), she is victimized by a constant need for affirmation from external sources. Sadly, such legitimation is only temporarily soothing. If one has been discouraged from pursuing one's authentic wishes, one has little experience of the feeling of genuine satisfaction and contentment. Women's frequent, and often frantic, pursuit of conformity with the ever-changing aesthetic demands of the beauty industry can be understood in part to depend on the development of a feminine psychology just described.

Over and above the specific injunctions that mothers transmit to their daughters, another side of the consequences of our parenting arrangements needs to be brought into the picture in order for us to understand yet another strand in the complex of psycho-social forces that at once create a body insecurity in women and frustrate its adequate resolution. We need to understand the culture's fascination and fear of women as expressed through the desire to control women's bodies.

Current child-rearing arrangements in which women mother, ensure that the power of the mother is deeply embedded in each of our psychologies. The mother is the person to whom the baby most closely relates. The mother's body provides nourishment and comfort for the baby, and the mother's physical presence provides a sense of containment for the developing child.[9] In the process of the psychological birth of the human infant, in which it mopes from utter dependence to separation–individuation, the mother's psychology is "taken in" by the developing person and forms the very core of his or her personality.[10] During the first year of life, the mother is a most powerful presence in a number of ways. She is the mediator for the baby's experience, her actions organize the stimuli that flow between the baby and the world and the world and the baby.[11] She relates to the baby and its needs—sometimes she is able to meet them and sometimes she is not. Her steady presence in the baby's life means that she comes to represent, in their most basic forms, good experiences and bad experiences. The baby is unable to control or comprehend the actions of its mother and is rather the recipient of positive or negative experiences in her orbit. Thus the mother, the seeming provider of such experiences, renders one either helpless or joyful.

In the first year of life, although the baby is thought to be engaged in an enormous amount of internal mental activity, it is physical relating—being held, fed, changed, hugged, rocked—which is the arena where mother and child most obviously meet. The mother's physicality is constantly felt both in its presence and, as the baby begins to differentiate, in its absence and presence. The mother's body seems to provide or withhold comfort, and as I have pointed out, the baby is vulnerable in this relationship. She or he may influence the mother's actions, but helpless and needy, is unable to control or direct them. Dinnerstein[12] has argued that the child's inability to "control" its mother leads to a splitting mechanism in which the "good" and "bad" aspects of the mother's relating become both internalized and projected on to all women. She draws bold conclusions from this by positing a kind of mass internalized misogyny. Girls in identifying with their same-sexed mothers distrust their own power, and "good" and "bad" parts. In the separation process boys attempt to repudiate their own femininity and primary identification with their mother and repress their own "good" and "bad" parts. In later life, they fear closeness with women because it brings up their own repressed feminine identity. In addition they project on to women (their wife and lovers, as well as women in general) the "good" and the "bad." They attempt to control what they could not earlier. They reject the power of the mother through the political and psychological subjugation of women.

Although I have some minor disagreements with Dinnerstein's analysis, I think that in broad outline it provides a useful model which I should like to extend to explain the cultural propensity to control women's bodies. Paradoxically, it is woman's body that provides for her biological power, her capacity to reproduce. In our culture this capacity is both denigrated and exploited. The patriarchal

and state control over reproduction and sexuality, alongside the denial of women's natural body shape, suggests
that fear of the female body is immense. To take Dinnerstein's thesis a step further, then, one can argue that the
current child-rearing arrangements create in both boys and
girls, men and women, conditions of fear and, at the same
time, a desire for contact with women. The mother's body,
once the symbol of comfort and succor, is repudiated out
of desperation, for it defies the control that the omnipotent
infantile part of the personality desires so strongly. In turn,
a collective attempt to control the female form is expressed
in the objectified relations both sexes have towards wom-
en's bodies. The desire to control the mother is somewhat
assuaged by the control exercised over female reproduction, sexuality and aesthetics.

Before I move on to discuss some specifics about wom-
en's body-image and the development of anorexia, we need
to take note of women's experience of female sexuality.
As in all other topics we have been discussing, the Western norms vis-à-vis female sexuality in the period following the Second World War have been in a state of flux.
During the war a kind of permissiveness emerged, and
with the threat of men disappearing for years or perma-
nently, some of the pre-war taboos and stereotypes of the
good (virginal) versus the bad (sexual) woman were dissipated. With the re-emergence of the family in the late
1940s and 1950s, faithfulness, on the part of wives, was
the ideology if not the practice of the day, and virginity
until marriage was a moral value. Lesbianism was presumed not to exist. The marriage bed was just another
place where women were to please their husbands and look
after their needs. Satisfaction would be received through
identification with their husband's pleasure. Men in turn
were to satisfy their wives, but quite what that meant was
never too clear, and millions of women came to fake the

weekly or nightly orgasm so as not to disappoint or undermine their men.

Wives should not look too sexy or seductive on the outside, there were other women for that. Female sexuality should be contained in the couple relationship which was rarely portrayed as sensual (see for example the preponderance of single beds in the "master" bedroom in the movies of the 1950s and even into the early 1960s). Sexuality, a thread running through each person's psycho-physical *gestalt*, was seen as something women should curtail lest it threaten the established order. For, paradoxically, female sexuality was conveyed as potentially so very powerful that it was feared. Female sexuality both as an appetite and desire of the woman's, and as a spectacle for others, was conceived of as threatening. In the 1960s first the bohemian, and later the hippy phenomenon, challenged many aspects of closely held conceptions of female sexuality (in contrast to the playboy ethos). Work by Kinsey, Masters & Johnson, Hite, Sherfey, Koedt and feminist commentators,[13] served to open up somewhat the sexual options for women, but coincidentally this corresponded with another cultural tendency, the commoditization of sexuality as the ultimate object (see Chapter 1). The gains from the opening have had less lasting effect than might appear at first glance. Thus women in the post-Second World War period—both mothers and daughters—have learned to walk a precarious line in relation to one of the fundamental aspects of human existence—their sexuality.

To turn now to body-image and anorexia, we can see that the issue of thinness is one that has come to plague many women in the last two decades and that it is the dramatic nature of their response to the call for slimness which marks out the anorectic from other women. A dominant motif for all the anorectic women I have worked with is thinness as ultra-feminine and, at the same time, thinness as a rejection of femininity. In other words, two exaggerated and oppositional responses each representing an attempt to negotiate an individual's identity, operate simultaneously.

For Audrey, the slimness she achieved with her anorexia made her feel that she was presenting the image of someone who was just "a cute slip of a thing." She went about her job as a nurse cheerily, speedily and efficiently. Skating from room to room, she was a perfect busy little caretaker and nurturer, bringing a smiling face and pleasure to those who had little hope. She excelled, if you like, in the feminine skill of looking after others and making their lives as comfortable as possible under the most difficult of circumstances. Her care for her patients was joined with an aggressive stance towards the hospital authorities who were frequently bureaucratic and thoughtless. She opposed them in the most disarming way. They never anticipated that this urchin-like figure would be tough and demanding. She was never dismissed for being "a ball breaker" (i.e. a forceful woman who emasculates men!), rather, she was uncharacterizable in conventional feminine terms. She looked impish, even childlike, but she was strong. Audrey herself realized that this cute exterior with the punch was an image she wanted to express because she felt it gave her a lot of maneuverability. She could look one way and be another. She couldn't be held to anything. She was full of surprises.

Of course there were negative aspects to this little dynamo. Far from being in control of these different aspects of her personality, outside the job she was in fact compliant and listless. The control she felt she could exercise within a work situation eluded her in the rest of her life where she had the most enormous difficulties discovering what she wanted and then fighting for herself. Like many, many women, Audrey could see what someone else needed and she could quite determinedly fight on *another's* behalf. She was a tremendous champion of the rights of others but absolutely hopeless when it came to recognizing her own needs or allowing herself to act on them.

Lisa's thinness was to quite some extent a rejection of her class background, an attempt to avoid looking like the cozy, overweight, housewifely women she grew up with, to project instead some mystery about who she was. In achieving the level of thinness that made her look as though she had stepped out of the pages of *Vogue*, she divorced herself from the image of her class (lower-middle by occupation and self-placement). However, she could not conjure up a feminine image that was any the less stereotyped. In essence her adaptation was an exaggeration of femininity. Femininity, as represented by mannequin thinness, meant for her beauty and untouchability. She wanted to become the kind of woman who was so perfect, so beautiful that she would not be tied to domesticity. She would live the life of an adored consort. She wanted to rise above the experience of the great mass of ordinary women and use her body to get power and protection. She saw herself rich enough to do anything she desired. She could be unconventional precisely because she'd been so successful at "femininity." Her thinness also represented a sharp break from the bodies of her parents. She saw her mother as gushy, badly organized, undisciplined and "all over the show." Her father was experienced as overbearing and gross. In fact neither parent was unduly fat, being within 20 lbs. (9 kg) or so of average size. Nevertheless Lisa's thinness felt like a real break with the values her parents seemed to embody.

Meanings such as these when investigated further often uncover other contradictory themes. In wishing to be able to control the outlines of one's physical appearance the woman is attempting to subvert a "natural" process—to change something fundamental about the female form. Even though the influences of fashion and current aesthetics impose that demand to some extent on all women, it is really only in the anorectic pursuit of thinness that this tendency to overturn so thoroughly what is associated with the female form is fully expressed. As the anorectic becomes thinner and thinner so she loses the definition that fleshy hips or breasts give. From afar she might not even be taken for a woman. Up close she is a subject for scrutiny, for her shapelessness removes her from the immediate categorization of conventional femininity. She is oddly desexualized and degendered. She demands to be related to originally. Reflexive responses—for example, flirtatious or patronizing ones from men, or the "once over" from another woman who needs to position herself vis-à-vis this woman—are confounded. She defies easy, comfortable definition.

Many women who develop anorexia talk about how they originally sought thinness in order to feel acceptable. Acceptance may have at first meant fitting in, looking nice, attracting admirers, in essence being noticed for being sexually attractive. Thus one might imagine that at some point the woman feels she is slim enough to win that acceptance. But of course acceptability, while attached in one way to notions of thinness and fatness, has in fact little to do with the inner feelings of acceptability which drive the individual to seek acceptance through extreme physical transformation. The attempt to find acceptance through conforming to a body-image is elusive and fruitless. And as the anorectic follows the pursuit to greater extremes, the response engendered is more frequently one of surprise and even horror for what the woman has done to herself. The thinness that the anorectic achieves is not attractive or acceptable, but rather off-putting. To be sure, it attracts attention, but not the kind of attention the woman thought she wanted.

Another example of what happens with the original aim to be acceptable can be seen in the case of women who were shy and retiring at a more average size, and became thin as a way to gain more confidence. Rather than making such a woman more "attractive," anorectic thinness keeps her in retreat, but in a way that magnetizes others. She is now looked at, not as someone who is appealing, but as somebody one cannot take one's eyes off. The attention attracted is of a vaguely morbid nature. The thinness becomes disagreeably fascinating and intriguing. Thus the anorectic woman gains attention of an altogether different nature than that to which she originally aspired. Now it is her invisibility that makes her remarkable. Now she has a presence larger than her size. A presence which demands a response rather than a reflex.

A stated conscious goal of the anorectic woman is what Bruch calls the "relentless pursuit of thinness."[14] But the satisfaction of achieving the goal is denied the anorectic, for she is never able to recognize that she is, in fact, thin. The thinness achieved is not felt to be adequate, or even if it is, it may not contain in her mind's eye a sufficient latitude for her to relax in the knowledge that she is thin enough. She still sees herself as someone large or potentially large. The achievement of the thinness cannot be internally acknowledged and the striving to be thinner continues full steam ahead. While this is an extreme response, it has aspects in common with many women's experience of feeling unsure in their bodies and full of worry about whether their bodies are all right. But to understand the deep distrust that the anorectic woman experiences and the evident wish to disassociate herself from her body, to not be in her body or to exist as a non-corporeal being, we need to recall the developmental

issues discussed earlier in relation to the making of a
woman's psychology and the forces which shape the
acquisition of a corporeal sense of self.

We have seen how in early development, the experience
of having needs met contributes to the development of a
positive self-image and a confidence that needs and desires
can be acted upon with a reasonable expectation of satisfaction. We saw how the development of a corporeal sense
of self is at one with the emergence of subjectivity, the
knowledge of oneself as a psychosomatic being, related to
other psychosomatic beings. Further, we saw that the
mother–daughter relationship, the critical relationship in
the forming of a girl's psychology, is shaped by cultural
(outside) forces and intra-psychic (inside) laws that frequently preclude the mother's consistent and unambivalent
relating to the needs of a girl infant.

In modern psychoanalysis, and more particularly in the
British School of Object Relations as expressed in the
work of Fairbairn, Guntrip and Winnicott,[15] the notion
exists that when the person, the object, on whom the infant
relies for growth and nurture is unable to relate consistently to the infant's needs, the infant fashions a world of
internal relationships to cope with the disappointments and
difficult reality it experiences. Unable to condemn the
caretaker, who is still much needed, the developing person
takes into itself the idea that it is not the responses of the
caretaker to its needs that are inappropriate, but rather the
needs it itself expresses that are causing the problem. Thus
it berates itself for its needs and attempts to bury them,
creating a fantasy world in which negatively experienced
aspects of the caretaker, the bad object, are reconstructed.
The bad object becomes split into two images, both of
which play a decisive role in the inhibition of needs and
desires. One part becomes, in the words of Fairbairn, the
originator of this useful concept, the "tantalizing, excit-

ing, needed object"; the other becomes the "rejecting object." Both these internalized images of the disappointing aspects of the mother have impact on general ego development. In so far as real experience has been distressing, there will be a corresponding level of withdrawal from the world of potentially satisfying relationships into a world of internal, and thus object, relations. To some extent all people are motivated by the demands of their internal world and the force of their bad object relations. What differs between people is the extent to which the individual is gripped by that force. Those who have suffered more privation of required nurturance early on are on a continuum, more isolated and consequently more caught up in the relationships inside themselves than those in the real world. In addition, new relationships which are sought tend to take on characteristics of the original object relations, so for example a deprived person is frequently disappointed by encounters with new people. The contentment sought is rarely sustainable.

Accompanying the overwhelming presence of a fantasy life in these terms is the inevitable development of what Winnicott calls a "false self." The self that one has put forward in the expression of need is implicitly rejected by the caretaker in her failure to respond appropriately to those needs. The psyche then protectively develops a more pleasing "false self." The false self is devoid of the needs and the initiations which seemed to push the much-needed caretaker away, for it is an attempt to take up and meet the projections of others. So, for example, we have all come across people who present themselves as carefree and contented. They are eager to please and to be helpful. They have developed an exterior which belies their inner unhappiness. When we look deeper we discover that, for example, such a person's mother was extremely depressed and could not cope with the expression of sad feelings on the part of others. Growing up, then, the apparently contented person received little or negative attention when she showed her sadness. She buried it and learned instead to be cheery and put on a good face. Inevitably the false self that is taken on is an alienated self, but at the same time it is the only self the person comes to be in touch with, for the unnurtured real self has been split off and repressed.

I think it is possible to extend Winnicott's formulation of the "false self" to apply to the taking on of what we might understand as a "false body." In other words, where the developing child has not had a chance to experience its physicality as good, wholesome and essentially all right, it has little chance to live in an authentically experienced body. A false body is then fashioned which conceals the feelings of discomfort and insecurity with regard to the hidden or undeveloped "inner body." The "false body" is, like the "false self," precarious. It works as a defense against the unaccepted embryonic real body. Again, like the false self, it is malleable. In attempting to gain external acceptance, the "false body" is fluid and manipulable. The woman in the "false body" becomes used to trying to reform it along approved-of lines. It does not provide the individual with a stable core but a physical plasticity expressing a complex of inner feelings.

Palazzoli[16] has suggested that the anorectic experiences her body as a bad object relation. It is the dreaded concretized physical expression of the still much-needed but rejecting object. The body represents those negative aspects of the mother that could not meet the child's needs. Thus the desire on the part of the anorectic to shrink ever smaller can be understood as the desperate but futile attempt to destroy the bad object. The "non-ownership" of the body is an attempt to create a breach between the bad object and the real self. She is caught in a tension. The separation from her embryonic self is at the same time an attempt at protecting it and an expression of her destructive impulse towards it. The push towards the latter comes out of a conviction that the "real self" is bad, dangerous and poisonous. The real self has needs, and the mother's early failure to meet these needs are the proof of their "illegitimacy" and "the badness inside." The needs are what send people away and the needs are the reason that the person is not adequately related to. But since she does indeed live in her body, the bad object encroaches insistently, she cannot be released from it. The person cannot make such a clean break from a problematic relation. The person desires such a release but is continually strangled or plagued by its representational form. Thus the anorectic's body is not really hers, in the same way that the development of a false self cannot be said to be entirely hers either. But although the false self and the bad object relation that the body represents for the anorectic cannot be said to be entirely hers, they are at the same time all that she has. They are experienced as the most present part of the personality, with the false self as the presentation to the world, and the bad object relations representing the absorbing and critical inner world that has to be continually wrestled with. This was dramatically illustrated by Audrey, who at twenty-six and after two years of therapy talked about giving up the anorectic defense like this:

It would be a loss to give it up . . . (long pause) . . . It used to be my whole identity. Now it is not really me but even so it is a loss and the loss of something not even good . . . (long pause) . . . like a bad mother you don't need any more, a teddy bear, a security blanket . . . (long pause) . . . the anorexia used to be an excuse, like a monkey on my back, the reason I found for things not being OK. Now I have to give it up because I can confront me directly.

In Audrey's case, when she was able to understand that the anorexia was a much needed defense against the exposure of a very vulnerable nascent "me" she saw how negative her original object relations, and the transitional objects that had come to stand in for her mother, i.e. the teddy bear, the blanket, were for her. The comprehension of just how disappointing those objects in which she had vested her security were is a testament to the strength and determination for survival that is bound up in the anorectic defense. Finally giving up on the hope that the bad object relations could be magically transformed and provide her with the nurturance and acceptance she craved so deeply, Audrey was able to begin the process of developing a psychological and corporeal sense of self in which needs for contact, needs for hunger and other physical appetites could be acknowledged. Such needs no longer resounded with unanimous negativity inside her. She no longer punished herself for wanting.

In Palazzoli's meaning, then, the body symbolizes the uncontrollable love object that the person who takes up anorexia still needs. Allied to this meaning is another symbolization. At another level the body has come to represent uncontrollable need and disgust. The body has basic physical needs that arise quasi-independently. That is to say, the body indicates its needs for sleep, food, defecation, urination, etc. These needs are what regulate much of daily existence, and correctly interpreted in early childhood such needs are met in adult life without undue difficulty. Yet the widespread use of sleeping potions and pills through the ages, the preoccupation with bowel regularity and the existence of a variety of eating problems in large numbers of the adult population suggest that these physical fundamentals prove problematic for many people. Certainly one can surmise that in the person who develops anorexia physical needs have been misinterpreted, thus causing insecurity or worry. We saw how in Jean's case the physical event of her menstruation caused an alarm that resulted in her becoming fearful of what her body could do independently. Her response was to mold and control that body as best she could. She treated her body's demands for any kind of attention with severity. In her case and in every instance of anorexia that I have come across, the woman does not respond as one might to internal cues of hunger, satisfaction, sexual desire, or fatigue. Nor does the individual really know how big or little she is. To some extent these inappropriate responses are the result of a conscious act, but what propels such inappropriate responses is a lack of confidence in one's physicality. In other words, we can conclude that the corporeal sense of self was not surely enough established. In the woman's history, doubtless her initiations towards food were misinterpreted.

In Laura's case, for example, the question of hunger simply never arose at the family dinner table. Dinner was held at the same time every night and Laura's mother portioned out the amounts she felt were adequate. Second helpings were discouraged (except for father) and there was a family ethic of moderation where food was concerned. Father's "indulgence" was remarked on disparagingly every night. Beyond the specific limits set on food intake in the family, the same kind of restraint on other kinds of desire and initiation was evident. The mother had been a seamstress before her marriage and had always wanted to be a dress designer. This activity was outside the customary route for a woman of her class, generation and ethnic background, so she devoted herself to becoming a good mother and raising the five daughters in the family. Laura's mother had had to suppress her own ambitions quite brutally and she had tried to save her daughters from this fate by bringing them up without any. She had encouraged them not to think of themselves as people who would work outside the home, but to model their lives on hers. She wished to spare them the disappointment she had lived with for so many years, by not stimulating their desires to express themselves in the first place.

But things had changed since she married, opportunities for girls were growing and Laura (the eldest daughter), who became anorectic, developed, late in her twenties, a strong wish to design and went back to college after working at a series of cooking jobs. The recognition of this desire was accompanied by enormous feelings of guilt and an uncertainty that this was really where her ambition lay, as she was so unused to responding to desires. Her anorexia developed as a way to mitigate desire altogether—to do away with needs as her mother had indicated, more successfully than even she had demanded. In Laura's case the wish to get physically smaller and smaller contained many paradoxical elements around the issue of need. One aspect the skinniness expressed was that in order to do something she wanted she would have to do penance. If she could deny herself in one sphere then she might be able to get away with acting in another. There was an enormous price to be paid in terms of repressing one set of needs in order to allow others to breathe. In addition, the getting smaller was an attempt to do better than her mother in the area of food denial, so that she could not be subject to the same kind of comments that her father received. In Laura's mind, if she could escape remarks about her appetite for food, she could "escape criticism on other fronts." If she withdrew from food, then her other appetite—for design—could not be criticized. The notion of dues to be paid was inscribed internally, like a balance sheet of accounts payable and assets on hand. She was constantly having to build up enough in the asset ledger so that she could spend on what she wanted to do. In fact in Laura's case, unlike that of many women who came to repress all manner of needs through the medium of anorexia, she did have a keen sense of things that she wanted for herself. The anorexia served as a limit on going after those things or at a very minimum made the path extremely fraught. The thinness that came from Laura's withdrawal from food expressed both a fragility about pursuing her objectives because she was so very hungry and weary all the time, as well as a strength and a defiance that she would do what she needed to do at any cost.

In the therapy, a crucial theme that needed to be worked on was her guilt at abandoning her mother's conception of the life she would have which, to Laura, meant abandoning and condemning her mother. In the initial stages of the therapy relationship she very much needed to be able to feel the support of another woman—the therapist—who respected her desires to be productive in the world of design but who did not underestimate the difficulties the desire itself evoked. A worry expressed by Laura was that if she could not suppress, or rather override, her hunger, there would be an endless list of things she would want, not simply food and design, but close friendships and travel and a decent apartment and a lover. She was fearful of where her desire might end. She was unable to see these things as legitimate and understandable wishes on her part but regarded them solely as the expression of a greed that must be held down at all costs. The giving in to one need was quite sufficient. In time in the therapy, the massive denial that such a stance represented became slowly unleashed with a concomitant realization that her body was indeed skeletal and undesirable. She was appalled at the recognition of the attempt to do away with her body, and as she slowly and judicially loosened the controls on what she had allowed herself to ingest and began to take in several little meals a day, she began to come to terms with the idea that needs were something that might arise in her on a daily basis; like speech, they are newly produced as the occasion demands it. She was also able to make a connection as an adult that she could not as a vulnerable child solely dependent on her mother—that a need not satisfied did not mean that she or the need itself was bad. It was simply a need not satisfied and was a result of circumstance, not a proof of her insatiability and greed.

Both Audrey and Laura had lived through periods in adolescence when they veered towards the plump. These periods were remembered as humiliating and related to confusion and shame about their developing breasts, pubic hair and the onset of periods. The body's apparent out-of-controlness corresponded with emotional outbursts which were incomprehensible to the individuals and frowned on by the families. This characteristically adolescent behavior soon gave way to experimentation with sex and with a range of soft drugs (marijuana and hashish). Laura became pregnant at sixteen, and Audrey refused to come home for hours at a time or to tell her mother where she was. For both of them, as teenagers, these acts were attempts to establish a less stultifying identity than the one permitted at home. Each developmental stage requires appropriate limit-setting on the part of parents, and in some measure Audrey and Laura were testing their parents to see what they would and would not tolerate. Looking back on these years, they both noted their wistful longing to be helped through this period, and the seeming blindness of their elders to the childlike needs that still plagued them, which they wanted satisfied and from which at the same time they wanted to flee. The puppy fat or plumpness evinced for them the explosion of this need; symbolically, fat became associated with disclosure of need, and thinness with the suppression of it. In the absence of these needs being met, Audrey and Laura both buried the churning and chaos they felt deep inside, and then proceeded to try to do away with it altogether by exercising rigid control over food. In this way they hoped to control the chaos.

The enormous psychic feats accomplished by the anorectic in her attempted suppression of need are exemplified in another way in which she relates to this body that is, and is not, hers. A notable experience for many women caught up on the anorectic treadmill is the involvement in physical regimens of a punishing and extraordinary nature. It is not uncommon to encounter an anorectic taking two or three "killer" exercise classes in a row or working out for forty minutes a day on the Nautilus machine after a seven-mile run. An anorectic rarely uses public transport, not because it is disagreeable but because it is too indulgent. Strenuous exercise in increasing amounts is often central to the maintenance of a psychic balance as is the denial of food. It is possible to understand these physical efforts simply in the terms in which they are first described by the woman, that is, as the attempt to rid herself of the calories she has ingested and thus conceal that she has indulged by eating. But there seems to be much more involved in the frantic exercise programe than merely the efficient use of calories. In several instances I have been struck by how the completion of exercise rituals gives the woman a real feeling of accomplishment. The achievement temporarily counteracts the feelings of inferiority that the woman lives with so incessantly. If she can achieve such extraordinary feats on so little food, and with so little weight, then perhaps she is of some value. Sadly, these efforts have to be repeated daily and increasingly for the person to maintain the feeling, which is transitory. Nevertheless such efforts are in the service of attempting to look after herself and give herself good feelings in a way that is entirely within the anorectic's control. She is turning around the frail image of emaciation she represents to the world and defying the conventional notions attached to thinness and femininity.

## NOTES

1. In this context it is interesting to note that women have shown the capacity to cease menstruation and take on the appearance of pregnancy such that their bodies grow daily when they are not in fact pregnant (pseudocyesis).

2. Banner, L., *American Beauty* (New York, 1983).

3. It is interesting to note that while the Jet Set's cool angularity expressed a kind of dispassionate interest in the world, Twiggy's diminutive size made her cute and adorable. Does this suggest that class issues and control are still strongly at work behind thinness? Twiggy engendered feelings of approachability whereas the upper-middle-class and upper-class slim women convey that they are unreachable.

4. The *New York Times* Survey reported 4 December 1983; the *Observer* Survey reported 16 September 1984.

5. Mahler, M., Pine, F. and Bergman, A., *The Psychological Birth of the Human Infant* (New York, 1975); Spitz, R.A., *The First Year of Life: a psychoanalytic study of normal and deviant development of object relations* (New York, 1965); Winnicott, D.W., *The Maturational Processes and the Facilitating Environment* (London, 1965).

6. Winnicott, *op. cit.*, p. 244.

7. Spitz, *op. cit.*

8. Mahler, *op. cit.*, pp. 221–2.

9. Winnicott, *op. cit.*

10. Fairbairn, W.R.D., *Psychoanalytic Studies of the Personality* (London, 1952); Guntrip, H., *Schizoid Phenomena and Object Relations Theory* (New York, 1969).

11. Spitz, *op. cit.*; Mahler, *op. cit.*

12. Dinnerstein, D., *The Mermaid and the Minotaur. Sexual Arrangements and Human Malaise* (New York, 1976).

13. Kinsey, A.C., Pomeroy, W.B., Martin, C.E. and Gebhard, P.H., *Sexual Behavior in the Human Female* (Philadelphia, 1949); Masters, W.H. and Johnson, V.E., *Human Sexual Response* (Boston, 1966); Hite, S., *The Hite Report* (New York, 1976); Koedt, A., *The Myth of the Vaginal Orgasm* (New York, 1970); Sherfey, M.J., *The Nature and Evolution of Female Sexuality* (New York, 1972).

14. Bruch, H., *The Golden Cage: The Enigma of Anorexia Nervosa* (New York, 1976).

15. Fairbairn, W.R.D., *Psychoanalytic Studies of the Personality* (London, 1952); Guntrip, H., *Schizoid Phenomena and Object Relations Theory* (New York, 1969); Winnicott, D.W., *Primary Maternal Preoccupation; Collected Papers* (London, 1958); Winnicott, D.W., *The Maturational Processes and the Facilitating Environment* (London, 1965).

16. Palazzoli, M. Selvini, *Self Starvation: From the Intrapsychic to the Trans-personal Approach to Anorexia Nervosa* (London, 1974).

# 5  Hunger Strike

Anorexia is a spectacular and dramatic symptom. To encounter an anorectic woman is to be confronted with turbulent and confusing feelings. These feelings can be so uncomfortable that one is inclined to try to distance oneself from the experience by various means. Unknowingly one moves into the role of the spectator. A sense of bewilderment, linked with a desire to understand, shortly turns to discomfort. One begins to look upon the anorectic and the anorexia uncomprehendingly. Compassion turns to fear and a wish for distance; a need to disassociate oneself from the painful sight. The anorectic is rarely engaged with, especially not about her experience of anorexia. Turning anorexia into an exotic state, with the attendant labeling and judging, substitutes for engagement. By these means a distance is created between oneself and the anorectic.

This distance is sought because in reality, there is a painful continuity between most women's daily experience and that of the anorectic woman. Nearly all women feel the necessity to restrain their appetites and diminish their size. The original compassion stirred in us when encountering an anorectic woman is about this continuity of experience. But equally, there is a substantial and qualitative difference between the anorectic experience and the daily experiences of other women. For although both experiences contain the same attempt at restraint, the anorectic relation to eating and not eating takes on a life of its own. While many a woman may unthinkingly envy the anorectic her willpower and ability to withstand the temptation of food, may even desire to catch a small dose, she can scarcely comprehend how involuntary this food refusal has become. So in a sense, we can understand the labeling of the anorectic's experience as an acknowledgment of this distance.

The dual process of recognition and labeling creates a symmetrical split in the way in which one responds, then, to the physical presence of an anorectic. In addition, the often appallingly difficult feelings one can notice arising in oneself when with an anorectic, are in inverse proportion to the very powerful but split-off and repressed feelings of the anorectic herself. The woman who is suffering anorexia is unable to contain a wide range of feelings inside herself. Without realizing it she flings them out into the world where they are momentarily picked up by those whom she meets. Like the food she would feed others (and even seems to push on them), she "hands over" her feelings to another. The extent to which the anorectic is unable to hold on to her own feelings and experience them directly, is the extent to which she projects them out into the world and on to others. It is as though they are tied up in a package to be passed on to someone else. As she lets go of the package she becomes voided inside. Meanwhile, the recipient of the projected feelings has an impulse to retreat. This desire, almost a compulsion to bolt from them, mirrors the anorectic woman's distance from those very feelings in herself. The encounter can thus be extremely intense.

On meeting an anorectic woman one is confronted with

the spectacle of a woman who is starving herself of food. Her body seems to have shrunk, her gaunt limbs hang limply from a quasi-skeletal frame. There is something out of focus about her proportions reminiscent of pictures of famine-struck Ethiopian children. Her eyes seem to take up a vast amount of her face. Frequently her hair is limp and lifeless. Anguish and defiance combine in the most curious way to make the observer passive and motionless in response. There is a simultaneous desire to retreat and move in closer. The conflict renders one immobile.

By examining in detail our responses to anorexia and the anorectic woman we provide ourselves with an alternative to reflexive retreat and incomprehension. We develop the pre-conditions and the opportunity to understand and meet her. The scrutinizing of our own feelings provides a way into understanding aspects of her experience. The "enigma of anorexia nervosa" becomes less opaque. A plethora of feelings are aroused in us. We have noted those of compassion and those of retreat. But let us look deeper into the bedrock of those feelings to unpack our seeming incomprehension. Let us take on the straightforward, albeit enormously painful, realization that *to encounter an anorectic woman is to encounter a woman who is starving herself*. Before judgement, distance, or indeed perceptive analysis cause us to retreat from that realization, the starkness of this fact should not be allowed to escape us.

As we let this realization enter us, we are chilled. Our body reverberates with a "No." We feel impelled to reject the idea, to make the starvation into something different, something less. We wish to deny what we see; to mute our response. We wish to change the behavior of the woman. We are horrified if we seriously contemplate the actuality of the starvation. But we must confront and accept this aspect of the anorexia if we are to understand its meaning.

Linked to the impulse to repress what we see, is the

desire to change it. We feel an urge to act; to take over the
feeding of the person, to stuff her full of food, to control
the behavior which is causing us so much stress. We can
only cope with what we see if we can act. But we must
look full face at the fact that many many hundreds, indeed
many thousands of women in the United States, the United
Kingdom and Western Europe are caught in a process in
which they are starving their bodies of needed nourishment, not because they cannot afford to eat, but because in
their view, *they do not have the right to eat.* Eating will
put them in jeopardy. Food, that central matter which
makes life an ongoing business—food which is the expression of our economic development and social relationships;
food, located as it is in the center of our lives, so perfectly
expressing so much of who we are—has been turned into a
forbidden substance. This feeling that eating is in itself an
illegitimate activity manifests itself in the action of food
refusal.

The refusal that seems so obstinate and determined to
the outside, is a refusal born of enormous effort. The effort
is required because the anorectic has to turn the meaning
of food around inside her. Food which is usually associated in a person's mind as a positive force has to be,
instead, perceived as a negative one. The anorectic woman
has transformed the meaning of food in her life so that it
becomes designated as dangerous to her well-being and
survival. Just as eating for most people is fundamental for
survival, so not eating becomes for the anorectic woman
synonymous with survival.

It is extremely hard to come to grips with the fact of this
food refusal. But by taking account of our feelings towards
her and imagining ourselves in her shoes, the rebellion the
anorectic woman is expressing reverberates and we can
feel the strength that is bound up in the refusal and rejection of food. There is a force propelling that refusal, a

force that one wishes to overpower, a resilience which calls forth an equally belligerent response—a desire on the part of the observer to control. The extent to which one wishes to intervene and press food on the anorectic, is a measure of the strength of her refusal.

The next thing we may feel is a kind of coldness emanating from the anorectic. A frigid shield creates an almost physical boundary that we dare not, or know not how to, penetrate. It is as though she is wearing a placard saying "Keep Off." We are deterred in our effort to make a connection and we catch a sense of brittleness; as though all connections are continually being broken or in some kind of jeopardy.

This shield is manifested in any number of different ways. Perfection, disdain, indifference or oversolicitousness of the other, all act as presentations of self on the part of the anorectic woman. In one way or another they have the effect of putting the other off, of dissuading them from seeking further contact. If we can keep hold of this feeling we may notice a hunger and a desperation that lurks behind it. Shielding the broken connections and the unapproachability is a despair and anguish about relating, almost a deep inexperience about how to do it, how to make contact with another. The desperateness often a part of this despair may cause recoil or fear in the other, who may experience the despair as a voracious demand.

This inability to make contact results in an emotional hunger in the affected woman. The flow of give and take implicit in most relationships eludes her and she becomes hungrier and increasingly isolated. She is starved of the contact she needs. The inability to connect with others, to be available for social intercourse, parallels the anorectic's relationship to food.

For the anorectic woman there is both an active and a passive relationship to food. This is a complex idea. An

originally *active* desire or decision not to eat or to reduce
one's food intake soon melds into an experience in which
the woman feels herself to be *unable* to eat. At first,
before the anorexia becomes entrenched, it takes a tremendous effort for the woman to limit her food intake. She has
to be vigilant lest her desire to eat spontaneously overrides
the decision she has taken to limit her food intake to a very
small amount, or to a specific and limited repertoire of
foods. The food she refuses is food that she is indeed
hungry for and is food that she has previously enjoyed.
Anorexia is in no way about the loss of appetite (the literal
meaning of the term). Rather, it is about the massive
achievement of overcoming the desire for food. It is important to realize that the anorectic woman is actively
engaged in depriving herself. We can get a hint of her
experience if we put ourselves in the shoes of the conventional dieter who, for a week or two at a time, determinedly avoids the chocolate cake she craves. However,
we can only get a hint, for the anorectic woman does
not reward her denial by substituting one restricted food
for another that is allowed (such as a piece of fruit).
She resists entirely her wish for the food that beckons.
She represses her impulse towards the food altogether. She
does this hour after hour, day in and day out. In this way
her refusal so magnifies the action of the conventional
dieter that it is in another realm.

While the anorectic woman fears taking in food for
herself, she feels the need to be around it. Not eating does
not provide relief from thinking about food, for it is an
ongoing preoccupation. Her mind constantly measures and
weighs up what she can and cannot have, continually
revising downwards her estimate of possible amounts and
kinds of foods. She channels some of this involvement in
food into preparing it—especially desserts—for others. In
other words, she shows concern for the food needs of

those close to her. She cooks and shops for them, and
discusses with them recipes, dinner party menus and the
latest restaurants. She has a public way of talking about
food, while her own method of actually dealing with it is
kept secret. In this way she preserves her private involvement intact. At the same time her own desire for food is
partially met through the process of projective identification. She gives to others what she so craves herself. Her
need for food is converted into satisfying those needs in
others.

The food she denies herself and the rituals surrounding
foods are at first based on conventional nutritional wisdom
vis-à-vis weight reduction. The woman may start off by
resticting her intake of fats and carbohydrates and only
realize somewhat further down the road that she is now
avoiding protein. Things she hears about food and its
capacity to make one fat are folded into her eating, and not
eating, behavior. Thus she may have read that food doesn't
get digested as quickly if she takes in fluid at the same
time, so she makes sure she drinks separately. Similarly,
she may believe that food eaten in the morning is "burned
up" more efficiently, so the quarter bread roll that she
allows herself to eat is taken first thing in the day. She
becomes susceptible to all manner of unsubstantiated
"truths" about the "fattening" capacities of food. Numerous rituals can then get added on to the various homilies so
that she sets herself a series of tasks to fulfill before or in
between each mouthful of the little food she does eat. The
rituals and regulations that come to circumscribe her food
intake tend to increase in number, gradually taking on a
life of their own in such a way that it becomes impossible
for her to envision eating in a spontaneous way. Thus the
original act of deciding consciously to intervene to reduce
her eating soon becomes not so much a moment to moment act of refusal but rather the consequence of the

labyrinth of restrictive practices that in effect prevent her from eating. It is in this sense that I am saying that the anorectic woman creates both an active and a passive relationship to food refusal.

A woman who overrides her hunger and systematically refuses to eat is in effect on a hunger strike. Like the hunger striker, the anorectic is starving, she is longing to eat, she is desperate for food. Like the hunger striker, she is in protest at her conditions. Like the hunger striker, she has taken as her weapon a refusal to eat. Like the suffragettes at the turn of the century in the United Kingdom or the political prisoners of the contemporary world, she is giving urgent voice to her protest. The hunger strike becomes the means of protest to draw attention to the illegitimacy of the jailer, the moral righteousness of the cause, or in her case, the necessity for action. She is driven to act in a dramatic and seemingly self-punishing way through the conviction that she jeopardizes her cause if she eats, just like the explicitly political prisoner. But unlike her fellow hunger strikers, she may not be able to articulate the basis of her cause. The hunger strike may be her only form of protest.

To situate the act of not eating in the realm of the political is to shed a new light on both the activity and the plight of the anorectic woman. We begin to see the anorexia as an attempt at empowering, and the food refusal as the action of one whose cause has been derogated, dismissed or denied. There is an urgency and a strength in the refusal to eat. This is no mere passing whim but the action of someone either desperate, fearless or both. To subject one's body to the rigors of starvation—to keep it fed only to the absolute minimum required to ensure survival—is an act of extraordinary desperation and courage.

To see the anorectic's food refusal as a hunger strike is to begin the process of humanizing her actions. If we do not yet fully comprehend her cause, we nevertheless open ourselves up to the possibility of understanding that there is a cause she is fighting for. We can move away from our initial recoil, envy or disdain and try to enter into an understanding of her actions at a quite different level. While she may not be able to talk directly about her cause, we can begin to decipher her language. The text we read is the transformation of her body and her action of food refusal. A seemingly incoherent set of actions and activities begins to display the outlines of something quite purposeful. She expresses with her body what she is unable to tell us with words.

While situating the anorectic response in its sociological context, we need to pick up the threads of our earlier route and pose certain questions of a psychological nature to explain the emotional underpinnings which lead women to anorexia as a solution. We need to be able to get inside the experience of the anorectic woman to translate and decode the meanings of her food refusal. We need to come to grips with the implications of the patterns of voluntary physical starvation that so many girls and women are engaged with, and we need to understand the function of the arduous physical activity that so often accompanies the anorexia. In this we have to move out of the realm of the obviously or seemingly logical and look into the workings of the unconscious, its language and its role in influencing or determining activities in the life of the individual. In doing this, we need always to set the unconscious within its social context and to remember that its laws are subject to those of the social world in which it is created. The unconscious mediates the experience of the individual in his or her social world so that world can be accommodated in a comprehensible form. The unconscious becomes the mechanism by which the individual accepts unacceptable aspects of the world as she sees it.

The unconscious provides for repression, splitting mechanisms, the creation of defense structures and the development of symptomatology that arm the individual in one way or another in her quest to be in the world. Paradoxically, these very mechanisms often remove the individual from the world she wishes to engage with, but we would do well to remember that the development of symptoms is always an attempt to be of the world. Thus in anorexia, the inability to take in food and the taking on of ever more strenuous and time-consuming physical activities are not expressions of a simple desire to retreat from the world of social intercourse but are imagined solutions for the individual, ways of being in that world.

What do I mean by proposing this? Anorexia is an attempted solution to being in a world from which at the most profound level one feels excluded, and into which one feels deeply unentitled to enter. It is an attempt to be adequate, good enough, pure enough, saintly enough, sufficiently unsullied to be included and not rejected. It is an attempt to represent and exemplify the values of that world and through such conformism find acceptance and safety. At the same time, it is an implicit attempt to rise above the considerations and commonplace values of that world and in a sense reject them from a position of temporary superiority. Anorexia, then, is a psychological bridging mechanism designed to provide some way into connecting with the world. This having been said, we need to confront the question as to why the anorectic woman feels herself to be so deeply unentitled, rejected, inadequate, bad, impure and sullied.

The world into which women of the post-Second World War generation were born is one in which consumerism has become a form of relationship to self and others. As I have already discussed, the values of consumer society are proclaimed in the ideological organs and means of communication in our society. But although these values are externally developed they are not simply imposed on individuals. They come to be experienced as central or important values to the individual. In other words, they become the object of our desire and are felt to be an essential mode of self-expression. The relationship of consumerism to women and women's bodies is intricate. I have suggested that not only is it the case that women's sphere of activity has frequently been directed into consumerism, but that there is a complex relationship between women's bodies and the fact that their bodies are so very much both *commodity* and *object* for them in the world. The world allows women to enter in a circumscribed way, to occupy particular spaces.

Entering the world is predicated on notions of acceptability. Access to acceptability is fallaciously offered through encouraging women to engage in the act of constantly perfecting their bodies. Columnists, advice columns, radio programs and television in which we see "real life" enacted seemingly offer pointers into gaining this crucial acceptability. However, the accompanying advertising copy, purporting to reflect "real life," has the effect of simultaneously undermining individuals" capacity to feel good within themselves without product x or y. For women the products most frequently relate to improvements to be made to body parts. The body is carved up by the various manufacturers who insist on the fallibility of nature and the essentiality of their product for improvement. As a result, nearly all women are subject to feeling complicated about their bodies and caught up in feelings of insecurity or discomfort to some extent or another. The anorectic woman, or rather the woman who finds an anorectic response, is in a sense echoing or proclaiming in an extreme form the actions, the fears, concerns, desires, hopes and wishes of women in general. The anorectic's attempts to change her body are in essence an exaggeration of the activities of all women who must enter a society in which they are told that not only is their role specifically delineated, but success in that role relates in large part to the physical image they can create and project.

The fact that women come to take up the call of manufacturers and the allied forces arrayed against them in the form of the advertisers, the beauty editors, the exercise teachers, the fashion industry and so on, addresses a more fundamental question in women's psychology. For in order that women should be receptive to the dismembering of their bodies there must be a pre-existing state of discomfort with and within their bodies, a profound alienation. In the last chapter, I discussed how a corporeal sense of self is achieved hand-in-hand with the development of psychological selfhood. I suggested that both these states were problematic to achieve, given current child-rearing practices and the psychology of femininity that mothers are vested with passing on to their daughters. I suggested that for many women, feelings of emptiness fill the space where one might otherwise anticipate the psychosomatic unity that constitutes the sense of oneself as a person. I discussed in what ways the mother–daughter relationship perpetuates a complex legacy in which nearly all women, mothers and daughters are bound to feel at some level that their needs, their desires, indeed their very selves, are profoundly wrong.

This sense of oneself as wrong, as unentitled and at the same time needy, forms a core set of feelings that all women come to cope with to some extent or another. For some, these painful feelings are but faintly heard at background level. While they shape the individual woman's struggle to be expressive, they are not *felt* as hindrances to the development of self. For other women, these underlying feelings about themselves produce a nagging insecurity and self-doubt. They prevent the development of self-confidence, they act as a brake on self-expression. They provide the ground from which defense structures are created and for which the perceived fix is self-improvement by the various means I have described. In the case of the anorectic woman, this core set of feelings obliterates (almost) all positive feelings. Self-esteem is chronically absent; indeed, for many women, the experience of oneself as a *subject* with feelings, rights, wants and the capacity to act is missing. In the place of self-esteem, a whole host of judgments and criticisms attempt to fill the void, to provide an ongoing sense, albeit a brutally negative one, of existence. Lacking an internal sense of solidity or continuity, the psyche has erected a way (essentially a defense structure) to keep going. The threads that hold the embryonic person together are the skeins of punishment and self-criticism. Having not enough good inside to rely on, the woman pieces together an internal world replete with judgment and punitive rejection. Thus she flees these feelings of emptiness while simultaneously explaining to herself the reason for her emptiness. She is not good enough to get. She is unworthy of getting.

The same forces that combine to make her feel empty, unworthy and needy also stand in the way of her developing the legitimacy to be an active and motivated person. The initiatives she has wished to undertake have often been met with inconsistent responses ranging from support to disapproval. This inconsistency is incomprehensible and can only be understood in its crudest form, as a negation of the very act of initiating itself. Acting spontaneously, acting out of desire, acting *for* oneself, all become associated with doing wrong.

We are now getting closer to understanding what the anorexia is about. We are beginning to be able to see the outlines of the hunger strikers' cause. We see the necessity of creating a valued and active self. The denial and negation are the instruments for the creation of an apparently needless self—a self that has the possibility of being accepted. The self that one is, is demonstrably not acceptable, and the alternatives are to break down entirely or to change that self. Survival is conceived of in terms of changing the self, and survival depends upon putting the cause of creating an acceptable self on the agenda. The self that one has put forward, a self with needs and wants, has been rejected. Thus a self without such problematic needs must be created. And so the woman takes on the cause of creating out of herself a new persona, a new self that, stripped of needs and desire, will find more acceptance in the world, a self that neither she nor others will scorn. Systematically and ruthlessly, she counterposes her needs with deprivation. It becomes imperative that she successfully inhibit and control their free expression. The reward of gaining positive self-esteem beckons. This becomes the motivating force for the constant denial she engages in.

At first she is able to garner some self-esteem through the creation of this new self (the Winnicottian "false self"). She can feel some relief in overriding her needs and admire her capacity to be so seemingly need-free. She has begun to win the battle to control aspects of the self and in so doing she is temporarily buoyed up. In denying herself food, she rises above that most essential of all needs, the need for nourishment to repair the cells, to keep on going, to provide health, vitality and energy. As she rigorously restricts her intake, she provides her own vitality (literally life-giving energy) on far less than even she imagined to be possible. She discovers that she can take on an increasing number of arduous physical tasks without collapsing. She overrides her need for sleep, she pushes her body to run several miles a day or to exercise for hours on end. She is secretly proud of her ability to do all this and more, on an increasingly small amount of food. Needs and desires take on a distasteful hue and she begins to conceive of emotional and physical appetites as somehow ugly, even repulsive. She begins to derive a certain pleasure from being able to withstand and overcome the feelings that arise in her body telling her that she is hungry. Feeling the hunger is reassuring for it is a measure of her achievement. She can endure the headaches that follow. She can cope with the sleeping difficulties her famished body precipitates. She has started life all over again. The rules are all changed around. She will win a place in the world, she will gain a measure of self-acceptance as she practices self-denial and lives out the life of a person with no needs.

We can begin to see, then, that the cause she has taken on is that most precious one: the creation of a safe place in the world. She is trying to legitimate herself, to eke out a space, to bring dignity where dismissal and indignity were rife. Her cause is no less imperative than that of the overtly political hunger striker. The resolve of her commitment is equally intense. The political prisoner who embarks upon a hunger strike does so to draw attention to the injustice of her or his incarceration and the righteousness of her or his cause. The anorectic woman on hunger strike echoes these themes. Her self-denial is in effect a protest against the rules that circumscribe a woman's life, a demand that she has an absolute right to exist.

As she takes on the job of creating a new person and a new life for herself, the self-esteem so desperately sought is only momentarily felt. The denial *per se* offers nothing substantive. It fails as a reliable source of new nourishment. It becomes instead an escalating struggle to thwart rising needs. As any particular need is repressed, so it presents itself more insistently in another form. More denial is then required. And denial can be no more than a short-term fix. The craved-for self-esteem is elusive. It is almost impossible to consolidate. It seems to be tantalizingly around the next corner. With yet more denial the anorectic will feel at rest. An ever-spiraling code of nots and denial ensues. A list of tasks to be performed daily, hourly, is added to the denial in the desperate attempt to get this new person right. If enough is done and not done, she will be accepted, she will have a place in the world.

The reflexive denial and list of things to be accomplished swells to take up the life of the woman. Paradoxically, the rituals bind and constrict her. The hoped-for goal of denial—freedom—is unattainable. The result is a frenzied attempt at yet more of the same. By an internal logic, they generate still more denial and more ritual. She becomes trapped in a seemingly incomprehensible maze of her own making. Knowing no way out, fearing the loss of the precarious control she exercises, she slavishly enacts the demands she has set up for herself. As her despair about finding the safe resting-place increases, so the method she pursues to find it intensifies. She loses sight of any goal and purpose in the relentless struggle to keep on top of all her internally constructed obligations.

The hard work of denial and following the rituals acts like a coat of armor between the woman and her inner self, and the woman and the outer world. Her painful inner experience of emptiness, despair, self-loathing and unentitlement is shielded from view. She disengages with both the original distress and with its source. In this way she is divorced from the possibility of another insight into its cause. She is convinced of the wrongness of her needs. Unconsciously she fights to be accepted. Her anorexia is essentially a defense against the recognition of the emptiness, an attempt to deny its existence and to connect with the world in another way, in this case by accomplishment and the subsequent garnering of self-esteem.

Into the emptiness, she has inserted a host of internal

.dges, who if she could please would become new "good mothers." She has created, in effect, a world reflective of her internal bad object relations. In other words, what she does and who she is, is always an attempt to turn unacceptability into acceptability. She is searching for the right mix that will assuage her internal judges.

This sense of inner emptiness has developed because there is, in effect, the absence of an integrated ego. The psychological development of the person has been such that the minimal feelings of well-being, which provide the basis of self-object differentiation (the experience of existing as a subject within a world of other subjects) have not been achieved. Instead an embryonic self, unable to use the resources that the environment provides, is hidden behind a mass of defenses. We have seen how the emergence of a self as a separate psychological entity occurs through the process of the developing psyche's taking in both enough nurturance from its caretaker to be able to feel substantial inside, and experiencing enough support for "independent" initiatives to begin the process towards differentiation and separation.

At first when the infant is merged with its caretaker in an undifferentiated state, its caretaker's ego (and for our purposes this would be the mother's ego) functions for both. The caretaker provides for a psychological orbit in which the child can grow and develop. The food for psychological growth is the relating—the contact that passes between mother and daughter. The quality of relating is affected by the psychology of the mother and her capacity to make a connection with her infant. Many factors influence how this relating will go. For example, a baby who cries a lot can cause tremendous difficulties for the most patient of caretakers, but at the same time it can mean that a lot of physical contact occurs as a result of the mother's attempts to soothe it. A baby who is extremely responsive

provides a good helping of gratification to its caretaker b̲
it may also be experienced as a very taxing baby; a contented baby may either stimulate its mother or dissuade her
from interacting extensively. A second child is a very
different proposition from a first. A third child is different
again. Factors such as these are the constituent parts of the
relating that occurs between mothers and children.

The factors influencing how a mother parents are myriad. They depend upon her own experience of being moth-
ered; they are highly affected by the degree of emotional
and material support that she has when her child is born
and during its first years of life; they depend upon the
mother's conscious and unconscious identifications with
the infant's needs; they depend upon the mother's feelings
about the gender of her child; they depend upon the expectations that the individual woman brings to mothering and
her capacity to shift with the baby's changing needs. All
such factors, and the many social forces that create particular conditions and feelings towards the act of parenting,
are folded into the mother's situation and are important
elements in creating a fabric of relating. In so far as the
mother is psychologically present, she can provide the
conditions for the developing, and as yet unintegrated, ego
to integrate and reach selfhood. Being able to be in tune
with her infant's unfolding needs, she enables her to take
in the necessary nurturance that provides the latter with
feelings of well-being, substance and an internal security.
As a child takes more and more initiatives, the mother is
able to support them and by so doing conveys the rightness
of its desires and activities. In so far as the mother is
unable to provide a reasonably nurturing environment or
respond unambiguously to the child's initiatives, the developing ego, and hence the child's sense of itself, will be
truncated in one way or another. Defenses arise to fill the
gap where a sense of self is lacking. In the case of the

...man who feels empty inside, void of feelings, fearful of initiating, and lacking an internal sense of continuity and security, the self has yet to emerge. It has not had enough nurturance to complete crucial developmental tasks. The cause, then, of the hunger striker is the preservation of this unemerged self. The extreme behavior of deprivation serves to deny this unintegrated self as it has clearly been denied in the past, while at the same time it is an unconscious attempt to protect it in the only way the woman knows. If its rejection has been caused by exposure in the first place—for why else was nurturance not forthcoming—then exposure is dangerous and this part must continue to be hidden from view.

By now we can begin to get a glimmer of what is going on, to see that, at a fundamental level, anorexia is only tangentially about slimness. Of critical importance is the fact that being slim is usually the result of a form of *denial,* and one our culture values. To be sure, the anorectic woman will declare that her interest is in slimness, indeed when her diminishing size is remarked upon at the beginning of her anorexic move down the scale, she is bound to say that she is too fat, that you—the observer—haven't seen how large her thighs/legs/bottom/midriff are. During the period leading to recovery she will undoubtedly have to overcome many stumbling blocks about being physically larger.[1] However, while these concerns are real and inform much of her thinking, they are only a piece of the picture. They are the piece, if you like, that links her with concerns the general culture is preoccupied with, and in this sense they are a break in the isolation she experiences. She feels herself to share the concerns—even if more intensely—of all women.

The relentless pursuit of slimness[2] is, then, in this context, about the need for denial. It is about the gains that arise from the denial *per se* and *not* from the slimness.

Achieving slimness is an important factor. It is a visɪ
proof of the woman's success. But it is the achievemenι,
not the thinness, that is psychologically important. The
anorectic is so used to experiencing herself as unsuccessful
that her now obvious ability to wield power over her body
is a fantastic achievement. She has succeeded in making
her body smaller and smaller where, patently, so many
others fail. She has, in a sense, licked the dieting mania.
She has gone far beyond the—to her—relatively trivial
concern of losing 10 or 20 lbs. (4.5 or 9 kg) and has moved
into the big leagues. Her success cannot be denied, it is
there for her and everyone else to see. The achievement of
slimness is important because it is about a kind of mastery
so rarely felt and because this achievement is a result of a
psychologically deemed necessity—denial.

Secondly, the achievement of slimness is important in
the context of what fat and thin symbolize for the anorectic. Fat has come to stand for need, greed, indulgence,
wantonness, unruliness, a loss of control, an unstoppability.
Fatness represents folds and folds of uncontrollable needs
and the guilt associated with the satisfaction of those needs.
Fat represents the *exposure* of need. The ability to make
herself smaller and smaller is the direct expression of the
anorectic's success in controlling such needs and neediness. Thinness represents this in a positive sense for her. It
reflects an asceticism of purpose, a praiseworthy puritan
morality, a needless self. She needs no extra, no padding,
she can make her way in the world as a spare and independent character. She is untouchable, without needs, she is
not vulnerable, she cannot be got at; she is safe in the
knowledge that wanting nothing, she does not risk disappointment.

Fatness also represents the plenty all around her that she
feels unentitled to. The wealth of goods in the marketplace
are all deemed overindulgent. The clothes that hang on the

ks, the diverting consumer durables, the records, the food, the many cultural offerings such as movies, plays, concerts, operas, to be experienced, are beyond her psychological reach; she feels she cannot have access to them. To be sure, she desires to partake of them and has an appetite for them in the same way that she has an appetite for food. But just as she cannot allow herself to have more than a few morsels to eat, rarely can she let herself have more than a morsel of the widely available goods and activities, and her restraint acts like disc brakes on her desires. She quells the desire and turns the wish to have, to experience, to consume, into a disdain. In this way she provides herself with a moral position to bolster up the resolve to continue resisting her emerging desires. Desire to partake of what the world has to offer cannot be quashed in one mammoth effort of denial, for desire arises daily and even hourly as one interacts with the world. Thus thinness, and keeping up thinness, becomes the moment to moment manifestation of the capacity to withstand temptation, to divorce oneself from the world of sybaritic existence, as though the anorectic is trying to prove conclusively that she has no need of such excesses.

But the success she has so desperately wanted and has now visibly achieved, eludes her. She can barely take in what she has managed to do. This new, apparently needless person she has created out of herself feels precarious. She is in danger of evaporating and making visible her very opposite, the despairing, anguished, needy person buried deep in the anorectic's inner world. While the routines and the denial are on the one hand enacted almost automatically, the deprivation so overloads the circuits that she is in constant danger of breaking down. Maintaining the new persona becomes a full-time occupation. The inner self threatens to burst out. It requires more vigilant binding-up which is achieved by an increase in the rituals and obsessive routines that take up more and more of , time. Her activities become somewhat embarrassing to herself and increasingly incomprehensible to others, and so she becomes progressively isolated and caught up in the demands of her newly created world. The insistent demands of the anorexic syndrome, by which I mean the food refusal, the routines and rituals, the exercise and the thought patterns, combine to compound her isolation. Her desperate journey to find a solution to the bleakness of her inner world leaves her psychologically shipwrecked.

The frailty that underlies the erection of this false self forces her to conceal what she is up to for fear that when questioned, looked at or challenged, it will collapse. The secrecy also stems partly from the shame of being involved, on an almost full-time basis, in the project of making oneself into an acceptable person; of turning upside down the things one feels oneself to be. But more significantly, it is the very precarious nature of the project that makes it imperative that it remain concealed. If her intention is revealed, her project will be threatened. She will be scorned and ridiculed. The tools which the woman uses to make herself feel strong and admirable will be questioned and she will feel undermined. She is on such shaky ground in this endeavor that she cannot afford to have her way of coping challenged. The secrecy so often noticed in the anorectic woman is not about a willful withholding, but is simply an aspect of survival. It is an attempt to have something for herself, something she can feel good about and hold on to. She must hold on to this new self-image she has created at all costs.

This stealth is especially pronounced in the way in which she relates to food. In the beginning of her anorexic phase she may not be overly concerned to hide her food intake. She is not so skinny that people are alarmed at the little she consumes, and she can succeed at eating quite

small portions without engendering too much interest beyond
the routine praise and envy that surround anyone who is
seen to be dieting. As she and her food intake diminish,
special care has to be taken not to alert others to her
goings-on for fear that they will press food on her. She
begins to be able to eat only the little food she has decided
she is allowed to have on her own; she develops rituals for
ingesting that food; she has special times when she can
eat, and she may decide that she can eat only foods that
she has personally prepared. So for instance, Audrey's
daily food allowance (see Chapter 3) consisted of a roll of
sugar-free mints, 100g cottage cheese or yoghurt, two
iceberg lettuces, 500g carrots, three teaspoons of bran,
half the white of a small egg, unlimited amounts of Diet
Coke and black coffee, and a quarter or a half of an
English muffin.

Eating with others becomes tortuous. The anorectic
woman learns how to sit at a table and make the ordinary-
sized meal set in front of her disappear. She hides the food
on her plate under the lettuce leaves, or it lands on the
floor under her or someone else. Sometimes it is dropped
into a convenient handbag or receptacle of some kind
situated on her lap. She becomes extremely adept at flick-
ing food here and there without drawing much attention to
herself. What stays on her plate is assiduously cut up into
small pieces, thus she appears to be having the same thing
to do as everyone else at the table. If she does eat it is
usually the prelude to a binge, an uncontrollable eating
episode in which her restraint explodes into its very opposite and she eats everything in sight and more. She may
find herself going from café to fast food restaurant to
take-out delicatessen, cramming a wide variety of food in
her mouth—food she denies herself on a daily basis. She
eats more than an average meal. She may start with a
pastrami sandwich and a bag of potato crisps, go on to a

hamburger and French fries, bacon and eggs, a slice of cheesecake, a piece of apple pie, an ice cream cone, another piece of cheesecake, some celery, a banana, an apple, fried onion rings and so on. As we've seen, if she is planning to bring the food up, she marks the beginning of her binge with orange or tomato juice so that when she inspects her vomit, the red liquid will tell her that she has emptied herself. Under the most panicky of circumstances, she gives in to her desire to have food, but it causes her such massive anxiety that she cannot keep it inside her.

The stealth of the denial and the stealth of the ingestion are two sides of her experience. The conditions that create in her a sense of unentitlement to food at all, in turn stimulate a rebellion against this denial in the form of binging. In its wake the rebellion engenders feelings of horror for what she has done. The rebellion expresses the chaos, the screaming agony, the desperate neediness of her inner world. By eating this way she feels herself to be falling apart in messy little pieces, unhinged. She has partaken what is forbidden, she will only be able to reconstitute herself by ridding herself of what she has taken in. She must purge her body of the food and in this way symbolically cleanse herself of the act of having given in to herself. The purge is the relief of being empty, of being in control, of being back in one piece again.

The control over food and the particularly complicated way she relates to it is linked with a need to have something uniquely her own, something under her control, something she fashions. Throughout her life she has felt herself to have been on a path shaped by others. Who *she* is has been ignored and dismissed. She hasn't had a chance to develop herself. She has responded to the desires of others and tried to fit herself to their projections. Unable to do this anymore, she must do her own thing at any cost. She has designated her body as the arena for the struggle.

Treating it like an enemy, she wrestles with it, trying to defeat its needs. She puts all of her energy into trying to conquer it, to make it submit to her will. Paradoxically and tragically in this struggle with her body, she perpetuates the very denial of self that she is fighting against. But as we have seen, she gains a measure of self-respect and peace, for she has shown herself that she can be more in charge of her life than anyone else.

Although she looks extremely frail, she feels herself to be strong, to have defeated the exigencies of the body, to have overcome its human limits. Her 70-lb. (31.8-kg) frame can run 8 miles (12 km) a day and work out on the Nautilus machines, she doesn't need to respond to the unseemly appetites of the ordinary female body. While others consider her pathetic and in need of help, her own self-image is one she is finally proud of. She feels a strength, for she has become someone with no needs and no appetites.

The anorectic woman has absorbed from early on, but in quadrophonic sound, the very same message that all girls take in in their passage towards femininity. She has understood that she must shape her life in the image of others. She must be concerned with, and attend to, the needs of others. As she develops she must negotiate her own needs, her own desires, her own impulses in an environment filled with no-go areas and land-mines. Somewhere she has understood the danger and impossibility of being for herself. Her crime has been that she has felt needy and initiating. Audrey tells me of knowing she had to wake up with a smile. It was imperative that she fulfill her parents' projections. Any expression of upset or pain was illegitimate and terrifying to the family. Audrey did not develop the capacity to deal with distress, conflict or even ordinary unhappiness. These feelings were to be hidden. They were *felt* to be obscene, vulgar and overwhelming. They must not be exposed. In denying herself food and developing an ever-increasing series of daily tasks to be accomplished, Audrey is trying to keep down her sad and mournful part, assuaging the guilt that disclosure of these aspects of self engender. In effect, she is policing her emotional life. As she brutally denies herself, she is reassured and temporarily soothed by her success at keeping her inner experience from view.

But this kind of socialization is very costly. Audrey has identified the having and expressing of any but happy feelings with being all wrong. Feelings are bad. Needs are bad. Certainly, she is bad. She is always trying to make reparations, to rid herself of the feelings she designates as ugly and reprehensible; to cleanse herself of her appetites and wants.

Audrey and her anorectic sisters are caught up in a struggle to reshape themselves physically and emotionally. Audrey has come to have little faith in her environment and so she withdraws from it. Inside her head, hours and hours are spent caught up in the obsession. She not only reconstructs her body but creates a whole internal world which makes ordinary social intercourse difficult. Any anxiety, actually *any feeling that touches her* is shunted immediately into the obsession. She thinks about how much she has eaten, how she will avoid eating for the next few days and how much better she will feel once she has constructed a plan. In other words, she is diverted into her obsession where things work out all right. She knows the ups and downs of such thoughts intimately. She confronts the anxiety eating stirs up by resolving not to. She feels relief and is charged up by her renewed vigilance. But tragically she is only further away from the distressing feeling that triggers the obsessing in the first place. The feeling is not experienced directly and digested, and so the idea is fed that she cannot cope with feelings. The gap between her spontaneous needs and her ability to respond to them grows ever wider.

The angular and skinny woman with the large bulging eyes whom we have wished to avoid soon becomes an understandable and approachable human being. Her struggle for survival, her hunger strike, the cause she has taken on become increasingly apparent as we allow ourselves to engage with her actions. The universe she inhabits is that same universe given to all women. Her response is an inchoate political protest, her *gestalt* the indictment of a world which squanders that richest of all resources—the capacities, passions and nobility of both sexes.

## NOTES

1. See Part II for a further discussion of this.
2. Bruch, H., *The Golden Cage: The Enigma of Anorexia Nervosa* (New York, 1978).

# PART II

# 6 Towards a Model of Self-help: Themes to Be Considered and Tackled

A reader who, at this stage, accepts that she is anorectic and recognizes anorexia in its active sense as a hunger strike in the cause of selfhood, may be put off by the prospect of treatment as it appears to render one passive, an object to be acted upon. Such a reader might well ask where one might find a therapeutic context that honors the symptom, the client and her struggle. (Indeed, the next chapter will pinpoint the underpinnings for just such a treatment model.) In this chapter, I propose a set of themes, guidelines and areas of consideration for those women who wish to begin on their own to explore ways of untangling the complex psychological underpinnings of their anorexia.

The notion of self-help in the treatment of anorexia may strike many mental health practitioners as extremely problematic and unrealistic. Anorexia is a frightening syndrome. The psychological nature of the problem and the physical diminution of the sufferer is a deterrent to successful contact and treatment by even the most experienced health professionals. The very fact of starvation can create in the sufferer a mental imbalance, including frequent paranoid thoughts; the physical implications are no less grave, leading most practitioners to recommend hospitalization and a program for the immediate putting-on of weight. In addition, most workers in the field encounter the anorectic after she has suffered with the problem for many years. The syndrome is entrenched and the practitioner is only the latest in a long line of medical and mental health professionals the sufferer has encountered. The anorectic apparently feels little inclination to change; she projects a curious mixture of diffidence, disdain and dismissiveness. Inpatient treatment has a disappointingly low, long-term success rate, and new psychotherapeutic modalities are continually being developed in order to maximize therapeutic effectiveness. The experiences of those working therapeutically in a wide range of contexts with anorectic women provide few warming or hopeful accounts of the enterprise. Against such a background, what claim can self-help have to the aiding of the anorectic?

Self-help has a role to play in coming to grips with and the recovering from anorexia. It is by no means second-best to another preferable treatment but a route to recovery in and of itself. It will not be of use to all those who suffer from anorexia and for others it will be but a step towards, or an adjunct of, other treatment. Frequently, it will be of particular value during the recovery process when one has been able to break through a certain need for isolation and withdrawal, and there now arises a desire to join with others who have been anorectic. The range of people it will appeal to and can help will include those who have been disappointed by inpatient treatment; those who are inclined to seek help outside the parameters of conventional medicine, psychiatry and psychotherapy; and those whose distrust of authority figures is such that help proffered by others cannot be used. In addition, women who are influenced by feminism's discussion of the role of the medical and mental health establishments in the treatment of women in general may find self-help a syntonic alternative.

Self-help in this context does not mean a well-worked-out set of things to do that constitute an established practice. Indeed, one cannot codify self-help for anorexia in that way. It consists rather of recommended guidelines and areas for consideration. First and foremost, self-help in general—and this chapter in particular—will provide a context in which the woman who is suffering from anorexia can make meaningful steps towards a recognition of her problem.

Let me anticipate the comments of those who, used to working with anorectic women in dire straits, find the notion of self-help preposterous if not downright dangerous. Let me try to answer the fears of practitioners involved week in and week out in physical life-saving practices with their emaciated anorectic patients. I imagine that objections will be made on the grounds of the necessity of intervention when a condition is seen as life-threatening. The efficacy of such interventions are, I assert, untested and less successful than one would wish. The successful recovery from anorexia, as opposed to the temporary fattening-up of the hospitalized anorectic, is notoriously difficult. Few practitioners claim more than a scant success rate. The frustration that those working with anorectics often feel may raise a suspicion that I am suggesting we shirk the hard work of learning how to relate to the anorectic, and how to help her. That is in no sense my intent, for I believe such attempts must and should be made. The thrust of this chapter, however, is to acknowledge that self-help has an important role to play in the recovery from anorexia.

The first step is the process of recognition—the acceptance that one has a problem. Such a recognition makes it possible for the individual to begin to face the facts of her situation on her own, and to explore the possibilities and services available to her.

The idea of self-help is hardly a novel one. Neither is the actuality. Organizations providing a wide range of services for anorectics and their families have existed for several years. These services range from the straightforward dissemination of information about anorexia (and increasingly now bulimia), support for families who include an anorectic member, directories of treatment possibilities, counseling groups initiated by ex-anorectics, dietary advice and so on. The recognition of anorexia by the sufferer herself or by a family member frequently engenders panic about how and where to go for reasonable treatment. Organizations have sprung up to detail and describe the range of possibilities from self-help to behavior modification, or more actively interventionist models.

Recognizing that one is involved in anorectic ways of thinking is an idea that many women resist acknowledging. To acknowledge that one has a problem is to risk losing something felt to be utterly crucial to one's way of being. Recognition takes place most happily when it can be linked with the possibility of other ways of coping and being in the world. Recognition is an absolutely essential step in the process towards recovery. I use the term recovery here to mean the capacity to live a life free from the hourly terrors that accompany food deprivation, its associated ritualistic behaviors and thought patterns.

It is not possible to change fundamental ways of being and of self-conception, before looking in the mirror and recognizing who one is. One needs to take stock of the practices that have kept one going, and so open up the possibility of change. The recognition of oneself as anorectic can awaken a compassionate response towards oneself. It is important to be able to realize the dreadful denial and deprivation one has been and is going through, and the feelings of unentitlement that have meant that the environment is seen as malevolent. For many women the acknowledgment of their condition leads to self-recriminatory thoughts, judgment and yet more self-hatred—the very feelings which originally produced an anorectic response. So it is important that the individual use the recognition of her problem as the springboard to a different and sympathetic response to herself. Looked at from the outside, that is to say, reflecting on the facts of the deprivation, it is easy to see how a compassionate response is stirred. These feelings need to be harnessed in the service of helping oneself through to recovery. Often the experience of being with another women or other women who are coming to grips with their problems is useful, for a compassion that may be missing towards oneself is generated towards others and can ultimately reflect back on oneself.

The attainment of these compassionate feelings is important, for they begin to break through the robotic response of self-hatred. The feelings that the anorexia has been attempting to bind up—of anger, disappointment, loneliness, insecurity, emotional hunger and so on can come to the surface and be experienced. At first these feelings will be unwelcome, disconcerting, uncomfortable and distressing. They will be like ghosts from the past, disagreeable and emotional—like time bombs that threaten to explode. Habituated to repressing these kinds of feelings, the anorectic will experience a strong desire to retreat from them, to take on the familiar emotional armor and surround herself with the familiar patterns of obsessive thoughts and actions. This is most understandable, but in order to get through the anorexia it will be necessary to struggle with this desire and to overcome habitual responses. It will be important to take the breathing space to consider a different response towards what arises within oneself.

Related to this act of recognition is the need to confront the issue of secrecy in anorexia. As we have seen, the nature of the problem predisposes the anorectic to stealth. It is not simply that she hides as best she can her activities around food and routines from the eyes of others, but that she herself is involved to quite some extent in keeping from her *own* view the actuality of the practices—both the obsessive thoughts and the practice of self-starvation. This maintenance of secrecy is only partial for, as I have already pointed out, an important secondary gain of the anorexia is the self-esteem derived from the knowledge of one's capacity to override hunger and appetite. At the same time that this is an important factor for the anorectic, the psychological mechanisms of splitting and repression combine to distance and disconnect the woman from a real recognition of what she is doing. This doubtless sounds odd, but an example from everyday experience might explain what I mean more graphically. One has overspent the allowed budget and put a subsequent purchase on a credit card. One enjoys the newly bought item. A vague amnesia sets in as to amounts owing or even the fact of debt until the arrival of the credit card bill. One's awareness is dimmed or cast aside much in the same way as the anorectic's knowledge of her own actions.

It is this very need to conceal from herself the facts of crucial parts of her existence that makes self-help a particularly effective way for the anorectic woman to begin to solve her dilemma, for it provides scope for self-disclosure in a non-coercive context. For many women with anorexia, the forced disclosure of the problem before they feel ready, for instance in the case of a confrontation with a general practitioner or school counselor, further adds to the tenacity of the defense structure. Similarly a woman who might be ready to make tentative steps towards the realization that she has a problem, may be put off by the prospect of an encounter with a professional, for such an encounter itself signifies too emphatic a recognition. Self-help in which the pace is structured by the woman herself offers a useful way into illuminating one's experiences.

As the pace needs to be structured by those who are suffering from anorexia, a self-help model can do no more than suggest areas for consideration and themes that might usefully be explored in such an undertaking. Many of the issues which are discussed in detail in the subsequent chapters on treatment will be useful to those who wish to start up self-help groups. In addition, readers may find *Fat is a Feminist Issue II* useful in this regard as it spells out in detail guidelines for how to set up, organize and run groups on eating problems.

The three main areas that will need to be addressed are: (1) working on accepting feelings and needs; (2) taking the fear out of food; and (3) reconciling oneself to one's body-image. Having said this, since self-help obviously highlights the sufferer's experience, other issues will seem equally relevant and pressing to those engaged in trying to understand and change their responses to food.

In suggesting a series of meetings for like-minded sufferers which have a particular topic as a focus for each session, I am in no way meaning to limit the scope of such meetings but rather to suggest topics that may be useful in starting a group. Certain common themes occur in the lives of all women, and especially in the lives of women with eating problems. Having a chance to consider certain themes with others whose experience may be similar, validates that experience. It allows one to take feelings and adaptations more seriously, and to do so in a less critical vein than usual.

A useful place to start is with personal history. In these sessions, it will be important to try to talk as honestly and directly from experience as possible, because there is no sense in which anything said will be at all shocking to other participants. Indeed, openness in these circumstances may well be easier than anywhere else, for there is no threat that one's way of coping will come as a shock to anyone else in the group, nor is it likely to be disparaged or misunderstood.

*Personal history* subjects to be discussed could include: a sharing of the deemed commencing of "the problem"; one's own and others' awareness of the beginning of anorexia; attitudes of friends and/or family members to anorexia; what a typical day is like currently in regard to eating and non-eating; the course of the anorexia—including the various attempts each person may have made to try and get over, through or around it; discussion of various treatments one has experienced; helpful and unhelpful professional interventions.

Topics that might follow from this are:

*The role of food in the family and eating patterns of family members*. In this one might explore other family members' relationship and attitudes to food—is it generally regarded as pleasurable? Something to be scared of? For whom does it form a preoccuption?, and so on; other family members with eating problems and the responses to those problems.

*Feelings about food and eating*. How one manages food currently—both when alone and with other people. Is binging a frequent accompaniment to the anorexia? When was food, if ever, an enjoyable part of life? Difficulties with eating now—both worries about being out of control and issues of physical discomfort.

*Routines and rituals*. The daily or hourly obligations one has instituted. What they feel like. When did they start up? Are they on the increase? Fatigue and sleeplessness. Physical symptoms in general.

*Control and lack of control*. What control means. What

being in control or out of control feels like. What areas in one's life—if any—are free of the need to be controlled. What areas feel out of control or chaotic.

*Secrecy.* How being secretive makes one feel. Did the need for secrecy exist before the onset of the anorexia? Does secrecy extend beyond the areas of food and rituals? Is there a felt need to hide one's emotions?

*Friendships and relationships.* How open can one be with friends? Has the anorexia brought about social isolation?

*Dependence and independence.* How do issues around dependency and autonomy relate to one's life, and how are they expressed in the anorexia? Is there a value judgment attached to these themes?

*Body size and body-image.* Fear of fat. Distortions. Not seeing oneself as others do. Would any size be sufficiently thin? What does thinness represent? What does fatness mean? Body size of family members. Body size through the years.

*Sexuality.* How is sexual desire/experience affected by the anorexia? What feelings does one have about sexual contact, periods, pregnancy, etc?

*Inclusion/exclusion.* Do these themes speak to one's experience? Has one felt/does one feel excluded from peer groups or alienated and misunderstood within the family? What would inclusion or acceptance on one's own terms feel like?

The generation of relevant topics seems almost infinite. If a sufficiently supportive ambience can be created, then any issue that touches on any individual woman's experience of the anorexia can be talked about. The goal of a self-help group is to provide support, a new way to look at one's life and an opening to consider different ways to live with the tensions, difficulties and feelings that are bound up in the anorexia. The two most obvious manifestations of the anorexia, the fear of food and the confusion about

body-image, are the topics around which a group of anorectic women will find enormous commonality of experience. Since so much of the anorexia is an attempt at
self-respect (the solution to feelings of self-dislike, even
self-loathing), the experience of being in a group with
other women who are plainly not contemptible, hateful or
to be dismissed and yet think themselves to be—as evidenced by the fact that they all have the same way of
coping through denial of self—is extremely helpful. It
forces reappraisal of why and how one has come to have
such a low self-regard. It offers the possibility that one
will engender some sympathy towards oneself rather than a
continually punitive attitude. Being able to observe the
punitive ways in which others relate to themselves can
help one confront a similar response in oneself.

This is not being unrealistically optimistic about what
can be achieved by meeting with people in the same
circumstances, but it shows the possibilities that exist when
one is able to break down some of the isolation and engage
with others in similar situations. The experience of voluntarily getting together with other sufferers can act as a
catalyst to seeing oneself differently—as though one has
actually been able to look in the mirror and recognize what
is there.

In such an undertaking, the existence of an open atmosphere where everybody can contribute as much as they
wish without feeling that they will be judged, but rather
that their experience will be understood, is crucial. The
managing of feelings and needs, the pivotal area of difficulty for all women with anorexia, is obviously of considerable concern. In a group it is easy to observe in others (if
not in oneself) the damaging effects that the suppression of
feelings and needs creates. This recognition needs to inform both the content and the practice of the group. Learning to recognize and accept feelings and needs in oneself

and then coming to express them is an important general focus for any self-help work. In subsequent sections of this book, I have detailed some of the ways in which practitioners may be helpful in enabling those they work with to accept and express a whole range of uncomfortable feelings and needs. The suggestions I make on pp.204–231 will be especially helpful to those engaged in self-help. The guidelines about body-image (pp.187–202) and the discussion around food (pp.166–86) are also relevant to groups and individuals who are exploring their problems outside conventional treatment.[1]

## NOTES

1. Anorexics Aid, the Anorexia Counselling Service and various US organizations have existed since the 1970s.

Anorexic Aid
The Priory Centre
11 Priory Road
High Wycombe
Buckinghamshire
England

National Association of Anorexia Nervosa and Associated Disorders
Box 271
Highland Park
Illinois 60035
USA

# 7   Bridging the Chasm

## THERAPEUTIC CONSIDERATIONS: An Introduction

As I have attempted to demonstrate in the previous chapters, the upsurge in the incidence of anorexia is bound up in the particular circumstances of our times. This increase cannot be ignored, nor should we content ourselves with explanations or treatment models that fail to address it. To look at anorexia nervosa as essentially a physiological disturbance, a purely psychological one or simply as a sociologically explainable phenomenon, is to miss the chance of understanding anorexia as a metaphor of our times—an especially poignant statement of the way that the predicaments of life in late twentieth-century capitalism can be experienced by the individual woman.

Freud, writing on women at the turn of the century in bourgeois Vienna, was well aware of the fact that social influences play on the construction of the feminine personality: ''psychoanalysis does not try to describe what a woman is . . . but sets about inquiring how she comes into being.''[1] Psychoanalysis has implicitly recognized that the shape of a psychology and the psychopathologies that span the continuum at any particular point in time, uniquely fit women's lives. The work of Renee Spitz[2] or John Bowlby[3] with children in nursery care during the Second World War is significant in this context because they saw a widespread phenomenon—the failure of infants to thrive—as a result of the impact of the absence of meaningful personal relations, a condition resulting in turn from wider political considerations. In other words, the political situation rebounded in the psychologies of wartime children in care. Again, the recent widespread acceptance of the notion of the narcissistic[4] personality is not simply the sign of the hegemony of one particular school within psychoanalysis. Recognition of narcissism is only the most recent example of the phenomenon of analysts and psychotherapists observing in their patients distinct constellations of particular psychological symptoms during distinct historical periods. Similarly, the well-developed syndrome of anorexia is not simply the result of a particular psychopathology. While, manifestly, the anorectic response is an attempt at a psychological solution, the solution that is sought and the underlying psychology that makes such a response possible are formed with reference to a particular set of social relations—the inheritors and transmitters of the ideas, values, tensions and contradictions inherent in our culture. As such, any treatment model that is generated to address the rise in anorexia needs to take into account those circumstances and an understanding of the ways in which an individual psyche absorbs and interprets cultural values.

An important aspect of the ideology of psychotherapy is a presumed capacity on the part of the analyst to see the psychology of the analysand, undistorted by the prejudices that the analyst herself carries. Part of the therapeutic process is the open-ended exploration of the material the analysis renders, the idea being that the analyst does not have a preconceived notion of what will occur but will follow what appears live and relevant for the analysand. While this is surely a noble endeavor, it is, alas, not an entirely realistic one. The questions the therapist pursues, the intonation of the therapist's voice, the moments when the therapist chooses to intervene, and the areas which the therapist pursues for clarification, are informed by some sense of the direction in which interpretation or understanding can take place. They are a means of making contact. They are preludes to abreaction and so on, and necessarily reflect the biases and the conscious and unconscious concerns of the therapist.

In stating the obvious, I am hoping to draw attention to some of the problems that may enter into the psychotherapeutic process that make a real dialogue particularly problematic in the encounter between an anorectic woman and a therapist. For despite the fact that psychology is clearly rooted in the social, many therapists disregard this aspect of their investigations. They tend to see the symptom technically, as the manifestation of a particular psychopathology. Of course this technical mode is important and crucial to the therapeutic relationship. However, if in pursuing a therapeutic relationship therapists fail to take into account the social world in which the individual has developed, they will form an inadequate picture of the psychic structures of their clients. They will miss the further understanding that comes from seeing how clients' psychic responses reflect the demands of the social world to which the client belongs. This failure can be a function of seemingly minor distinctions so that if, for example, the therapist is of a different generation from the client, she may be less alert to the cultural influences that are available to a younger person. If she is from a different class, she may perceive the environment as more benevolent than it in fact is to her client. These remarks are not intended to imply that the therapist should talk sociology in the sessions, but rather that she should keep in mind the social world in which her client's (and her own) psychology were created.

As I have attempted to show, the pressures that all women experience are the same ones the anorectic takes into herself in a particularly debilitating way. Thus part of the work for the practitioner is to investigate how she herself manifests and copes with the various influences that are expressed in the anorectic phenomenon. Specifically, she needs to be aware of the critical area of how a woman relates to and in her body. So, for instance, comfort and discomfort with body-image, the tyranny of slimness, women as feeders of others, women's entitlement to food, women as consumers, women as objects and so on, are relevant topics for self-scrutiny on the part of the therapist. Such investigations will help her to be open to the nuances of an anorectic's particular experiences. In addition, these questions are important areas for self-engagement by the therapist working with anorectics because in order to treat anorexia successfully—and I shall leave aside for the moment the criteria for successful outcome—the psychotherapist must be in a position to live with what the anorectic is patently unable to do, that is, with the tensions which, in the anorectic, produce anorexia. As these tensions affect all of us to varying degrees, there is no sense in which they can be ignored or overridden. The therapist needs to remain constantly aware of her particular accommodation to the conditions of contemporary femininity, and to recognize the implicit tension in that stance. This is important because there is a temptation—one to which I have already alluded—to take over the anorectic woman, to direct her treatment, to control her and to engage in a power struggle. This is often a way to cope with the split-off anxiety that emanates from the anorectic. Keeping a watch on the sources of one's own tension minimizes the confusion about what is happening for the client.

As we have seen, the nature of the syndrome stirs up strong feelings in others, feelings which include envy, frustration, rage. Such feelings can and do lead practitioners to mislay their compassion and replace it with a treatment mode that at its best is ineffectual, and at its worst coercive. Continual awareness of the complex of social and psychological factors that come to be expressed in anorexia guards against such superficial kinds of interventions. In broadening the scope of the picture the therapist draws for herself about the world of her client, she is more likely to convey her ability to understand what has transpired for the individual woman. She is more likely to be able to maintain a compassionate stance and to indicate to her client that her experience can be understood. In order for an anorectic woman to benefit from psychotherapy she has to be able to feel that her experience is accurately described, compassionately understood and that recognition will not rob her of her anorectic solution—her way of coping before she has developed other more healthy skills.

A starting point for a successful therapeutic encounter must be a commitment on the part of the therapist to what might be thought of as a kind of advocacy for the truncated person behind the anorexia. By this I do not mean a speaking *for* the "self" behind the anorexia, but rather an acknowledgment that the symptom has a rich and complex meaning for the individual, that it is in a sense the mouthpiece for the woman and that the discovery of that as yet underdeveloped person is crucial in the understanding and undoing of the anorectic response. Many factors combine to make the therapeutic endeavor an especially charged one. The emaciated state of the woman may alarm and frighten the therapist; the anorectic woman rarely presents herself for therapy with an optimistic attitude; the literature is replete with the prejudice that it is notoriously difficult to "treat" anorexia. Thus therapists become as wary of anorectics as anorectics become wary of therapists. In addition, and perhaps most importantly, the therapist herself is bound to be infected with a mild version of the tensions that the client is expressing through her anorexia. It is in this sense that I stress how important it is for the therapist to have a wide horizon when considering the factors that contribute to the etiology, assumption and continuance of anorexia.

GENERAL AIMS

The general aims of psychotherapy with the anorectic woman can be summed up as pertaining to the three following areas:
1. The creation of an understanding of the food refusal.
2. Focusing on the body.
3. Restarting the development of a self.

These three areas relate to both topic and attitude. In fact a compassionate attitude[5] is essential to the therapy process but is less common among therapists working with anorectics (or considering working with anorectics) than might be supposed at first glance.[6] An example from my personal experience may perhaps illustrate prevailing attitudes. My work with compulsive eaters generated requests for me to work with anorectics. When I was first approached (c.1974) I discovered that I was loath to engage in such work. In reflecting on this, it became apparent to me that I was carrying around a set of prejudicial attitudes towards anorectic women. I thought of them as highly distressed and hard to work with. As I understood it then, their relation to food symbolized a nihilistic relation to life. It would be a struggle, a tug-of-war to be helpful. However, in the course of running workshops and groups for compulsive eaters I would come across many women with anorexia who did not fit my stereotypic image. Women turned up in these groups who were looking for ways to control what they spoke of as their "out of control eating." To the compulsive eater the anorectic's "lack of control" was more control than she had been able to garner through the score of diets she had tried. The issue of what control meant and how an anorectic can feel out of control when she has overstepped the very tight limit she has imposed, came alive in the groups.

In this way I began to see beyond the stereotype. These were women whose actions could be understood as expressing an energy and a desire for life. Certainly many of them were simultaneously depressed and quite withdrawn. And it is also true to say that they were preoccupied with how to eat less and less, they had a distorted body-image, and the level of obsession made contact a bit difficult, but they were as various, individual and substantial as any other of my clients.

Eventually I took on my first long-term client. Still hugely prejudiced, I agreed to see her as I felt that she was different, that she was "highly motivated." Through working with her, my remaining prejudices were confronted and forced to fall away. The experience of the anorectic was so much richer, and the process of working together ultimately so rewarding, that I could not square my experience of working with anorectics with my earlier views or with the attitudes of some of my colleagues who worked with anorectics. My client was the first of many women who have let me into the inner world of the anorectic.

The development of a compassionate attitude occurs in the real relationship one begins to develop with the anorectic. It rests on an acceptance of the symptom *per se*, a commitment to understanding it together, a search for new ways of being. It means that one has to make the effort to get to know the inner world of the woman, to put flesh on the caricature of the symptom, if you like, to receive the details of her obsessive thoughts and practices, and to be able to find a genuine respect in oneself as a therapist for the struggles of the woman that comes to be caught up in the way she is currently living her life.

The prejudicial attitudes that frequently obstruct the development of this compassionate stance arise, in part, from the pain experienced by the practitioner working with the anorectic woman. The work is demanding, it is a long-term project and the "rewards" are not experienced in the short term. Sitting with an emaciated and withdrawn woman can be taxing, and maintaining one's feeling of confidence in the face of her overwhelming disbelief that anything can change is hard work.

Added to that, a painful theme running through the psychology of each girl and woman I (and other practitioners) have seen who suffers with anorexia nervosa is what can only be described as a kind of self-hate. This is palpable and while it is usually discussed in terms of low self-esteem and little self-respect, I think those terms are finally too mild to describe the strength of negative feelings that anorectics have shared with me. Further, the low self-esteem does not conjure up a sufficiently strong image of the brutality of the anorectic's internal life. Yes, the anorectic is engaged in a struggle to gain some self-respect and self-esteem, and this is precisely the aim of the anorexia, but that is as a counterpoint to the powerful warfare raging inside. Her inner world is chaotic and full of horror and anxiety. Ghastly thoughts constantly prick away at her, depriving her of any equilibrium. She desperately tries to assuage these self-hating thoughts in two distinct ways. Through the institution of rules and regulations in relation to food, exercise, habits of work or study, she creates for herself a self-image which can counteract the horrible, worthless, meaningless person she feels herself to be. At the same time, the preoccupation with the performance of the various rituals are so time- and energy-consuming that they in effect cover up and temporarily contain her potentially explosive inner life. The ritualistic performance of tasks, physical exertion and food practices provides a kind of comfort and surety in a mass of emotional bonfires.

Self-hate is debilitating. Anyone who suffers it will do almost anything to disguise it. They may turn it into depression, they may seek relief through chemical means, or seek to remake themselves like the anorectic. At times, they may be so overwhelmed by these debilitating feelings that they project a kind of unattractiveness. They cannot help themselves. They present themselves to the world as they experience themselves. Sometimes the case they make is so persuasive as to be almost convincing. One temporarily believes that the person is hopeless and hateful. Being swamped by such feelings, it can be hard to remember that they are the result of a complex history that has created a particular psychology and particular defense structure. They are frequently the mode of expression for a whole host of other feelings, which include despair, upset, hopelessness and rage. If the practitioner can hold on to the idea that this self-hatred is a form of shorthand for the worry that rejection is always likely, then she or he can be of infinitely more help to the person. Self-hate superficially accepted as such has the effect of distancing the other from the compassionate stance so needed in this work.

## NOTES

1. Freud, S., *New Introductory Lectures: On Femininity*, Lecture 33 (London, 1932).
2. Spitz, R.A., *The First Year of Life: a psychoanalytic study of normal and deviant development of object relations* (New York, 1965).

3. Bowlby, J., *Attachment and Loss*, Vols. 1 and 2 (New York, 1969, 1973).

4. Lasch, C., *The Culture of Narcissism* (New York, 1979).

5. Although the treatment framework is different from the one proposed in this book, Steve Levenkron, *A Nurturant/Authoritative Approach* (New York, 1981) also recognizes the importance of having a compassionate attitude when working with anorectic women.

6. In my capacity as a therapist training others to work with anorectics, I frequently come across a fear of, a disdain and a dismissive attitude towards the anorectic.

# 8  Food: From Poison to Palatable

## THE CREATION OF AN UNDERSTANDING OF FOOD REFUSAL

Food refusal, as we have seen, is not a passive act but the outcome of much determination and resolve on the part of the anorectic woman. It is a refusal born out of a deep feeling of unentitlement to actual food and what it symbolizes: in other words, an unentitlement to what the environment in general has to offer, as well as to one's emotional life and one's own body. The food refusal is an attempt at reparation, at making good out of what is felt to be bad—i.e. oneself—by transforming the raw material of the unacceptable self into an acceptable human being. This, then, is part of what one meets when working with an anorectic woman. One encounters a woman whose sense of self and of her rights in the world are so severely in jeopardy that she feels she can only exist if she minimizes her presence and her needs. Although her actions give disturbing messages to others, for her they are about the difficulties she has in being in personal relationships. They are actions to assuage the discomfort of her inner world (communications in the world of object relationships). They are attempts to find an inner peace that will provide her with some internal reassurance that, having suffered or paid sufficiently, she can feel some entitlement to live in the everyday world with others.

As I have also pointed out, the volitional nature of the original food refusal breaks down beyond a certain point, so that many an anorectic woman finds it difficult to eat, even when she is aware of being quite hungry. A consequence of having initiated stringent food refusal is the inability to ingest food without tremendous discomfort.

The importance of these meanings and consequences of food refusal for the practitioner, the parent, the friend, the husband or roommate is in the kinds of interventions that can usefully be made. Most people cannot mentally imagine or absorb the dilemma that the anorectic woman feels herself to be in. They find it hard to hold on to the idea that she is both actively refusing food *and* unable to eat, without feeling that she is being willful, manipulative, difficult or plain silly. They are inclined to challenge her relation to food by encouraging her to eat, doctoring her food, watching her intake closely, feeling massively irritated that she will not do what is clearly sensible to them. Such an attitude, while understandable, tends to be ineffective in dealing with many anorectic women. The active intervention by another necessitates a purposeful secrecy on the part of the anorectic and the development of a whole range of stealthy behavior to hide the details of how the little she eats is consumed.

A more therapeutic and efficacious intervention can be made by the practitioner who is prepared to accept and deal straightforwardly with the woman's actual control of her food, and to work with her on the understanding that she will be continuing to control her own food. In my clinical practice encouraging results have been seen by this open "handing over" control of the food to the anorectic.

It acknowledges what exists, and paves the way for the open disclosure of the actual details of the woman's eating pattern. Not having to conceal what happens when she is around food, for fear that her way of coping will be taken away forthwith, she eventually reveals to another person the ins and outs of her intake, her schemes, her obsessions around food. The isolation which is the inevitable consequence of her eating behavior is now pierced.

This is both exhilarating and terrifying, for the loneliness she had found herself in is the result of believing she will never make a satisfying contact with another. Letting the therapist into the details of her eating, and non-eating, behavior breaks the painful isolation and stimulates her yearning for meaningful relating, a desire that she has systematically crushed.

Of course, the processes of finding out about her food intake, the amount of time she spends thinking about food and the myriad schemes she implements in order to avoid absorbing what she has eaten, present their own kind of challenge to the practitioner. It is essential that she or he have some measure of the quality and quantity of the client's eating experiences. In my experience it is important to find out about such things in the initial meetings so that food does not become a taboo area between the therapist and client. A sense of openness needs to be created early on in the initial session.

CLIENT: Well, I have a bread roll in the morning.
THERAPIST: How much of that can you manage?
CLIENT: Well . . . a bread roll, you know . . .
THERAPIST: Is a quarter about right or is that too much for you?
CLIENT: Well, sometimes I can eat that much, but more usually it's a half of a quarter . . .
THERAPIST: Can you manage the inside of the roll as well?

CLIENT: It depends on how I'm feeling. See, I allow myself
a roll a day, well a half really and I can divide it in a
number of ways. If I'm going to be spending time with
people then I prefer to spread it out . . .

The client goes on to talk about the various ways she
might apportion the bread roll and we discuss how she
feels as she eats it. We begin to talk the same language.
She knows I know just how little she manages. She does
not have to hide that from me and we can proceed on the
basis of trying to get a real picture together of what her
actual eating behavior is like.

I am interested to find out how she feels when she
approaches food, what shopping for food is like for her,
how often she cooks, how she handles food situations with
others, and what she does at conventional mealtimes. Of
course one can only get a smattering of sense in the initial
session but I am doing several things in this kind of
inquiry. I am finding out whether she has words for feelings, while implicitly demonstrating that it might be possible to have them. I am discovering what kind of variation
there is in her eating and her relationship to it; I am
opening up the notion that it could be safe to talk about
food.

We talk about how her friends, siblings and parents or
husband react to her eating; whether she can sit and not eat
with them or whether she has to engage in elaborate plans
to avoid eating or disposing of the food on her plate when
she is at the table. We talk about how she experiences
other people's eating and in this connection, I am interested to know the eating habits of friends and family
members and the role of food in the life of the family of
origin/the family she is living in currently or the role it
plays in the lives of her roommates. These topics usually
have enormous meaning for the woman and discussion of

them will extend over the months and years of working together. They are, of course, the very content of the therapy, but I am eager to raise them early on from the point of view of demonstrating the breadth of topics the client can feel free to talk about and because the topics themselves are a way in to talking about some of her most painful concerns. Within this context we inevitably cover the circumstances surrounding the onset of the symptom, the self-knowledge that something "strange" was surrounding her eating, the ideas she attached at that time to food deprivation, dieting, getting slim or however she conceived it.

In this process one is both respecting the actual practices that the woman is involved in, while beginning a conversation with another part of her. In other words, while recognizing the overwhelming presence of her preoccupation with not ingesting, a dialogue is in process about the meaning of food in her life and in the lives of others. This demonstrates the variety of meanings food and eating can assume.

As I have already said, a key feature of our working together is that the client should be actively responsible for her food intake. This may seem an alarming proposition for practitioners who are involved in food management, but the fact is that the anorectic *is* in charge of food and for several years she has furtively tried to resist the incursions of others. Out of their concern and worry, parents, educators and friends have watched and made suggestions about what and how she should be eating. Each one of these kindly made suggestions is experienced by the anorectic as a pressure she is unable to meet. She is in a kind of despair about food, but the intervention of others—focused as they are almost exclusively on nutritional considerations—leads her into further helplessness which she deals with by tightening her control over food, becoming even more terrified of what "it" can do to her, and becoming defensive. Recognizing that she is to be in control of what, when and how she eats avoids the fruitless power struggle that ensues when anyone attempts to seize control of her food intake. Too often an attempt to "take over" the food department for the anorectic results in the discovery of discarded food in drawers, on windowsills, in plant pots and other unobvious places.

Thus we recognize and acknowledge her control over food. Provided there is no medical emergency—and I should add that I consider a stable low weight generally outside this criterion—I make the following arrangement with the woman. I agree not to intervene in her actual food intake if she for her part can agree not to go below the weight at which we initially meet. The joint assumption must be (and I hasten to add this is not so readily believed at this stage by the woman) that we are looking for her, ultimately, to be a healthier weight, but for the present, the crucial therapeutic work must start. The woman as a whole person, that is, including her anorexia, must be respected. I am not aiming to act as a surgeon and cut out the offending behavior (for I do not believe this is possible). I am concerned rather to ease the symptom until the strength and tenacity of it dissolve through not being needed any more.

But more important even than avoiding the ghastly humiliations forced upon both the unfortunate woman, who finds it so terribly difficult to eat, and the unfortunate person who sets herself or himself up as keeper of her food, is the impact of acknowledging that she is in control of her food intake. To enter into a therapeutic contract that takes her reality into account, is rather like obtaining a visa to a country which one has only ever read about and can now visit with curiosity and openness. It allows entrance into her land. As she does not perceive herself to be on the receiving end of the attitudes of a clumsy, aggressive tourist who wishes to see things only in terms that they already understand, her territory (her body and her eating) ceases to be in need of constant defense from others. It is accepted and she can show you slowly, at first, perhaps always slowly, the emotional relief maps, the general and particular terrain and climate. By disclosure and discussion, she shares her world with another. As one learns about it, one is gracing it with a certain validity, honoring both the symptom and the person. Implicit in the action of the outsider with the visa is the desire to understand and interpret the customs of this world.

For many anorectic women who have been ''in treatment,'' controlling their own food intake without being in a state of war with others is a novel experience. The anorectic may be so used to projecting her own conflicts about what she is, and is not, allowed to eat on to another (the doctor, nurse, psychotherapist, parent) that she may well have obscured from her vision the intensity of the internal state of war that exists *inside her* about food. She needs to address directly her own conflicts and to find a way to live with them by understanding them until they can be adequately resolved. In this regard, it makes sense to listen quite carefully to the plaintive voice that from time to time asks advice of the practitioner on what to eat. It would be a therapeutic mistake to take this request at face value, for the question is more about a desperate unease with food, a recognition of not knowing how to and needing help to discover eating/hunger/satisfaction than it is about the wish to hand over control to another. It is certainly the case that an anorectic can come to feel herself to be so desperately confused about food that she desires to relinquish the struggle she is having, and have that area all taken care of. Indeed, many a woman has said what a temporary relief she experienced when hospitalized. The practitioner would be well advised, however, to hear such a cry as the indication that the client is feeling dissatisfied with her relationship with food. She is ready to let someone else in to discuss trying something a bit different with it. This is the resultant reward for the practitioner who has resisted taking over her food supply. The question is not so much a question *per se* but a means of keeping the communication going; a way of letting the other into the anorectic's world, an indication that she is no longer frozen in an emotional wasteland, a request for help.

Recognizing and owning up to her conflicts about food in the context of a therapy relationship is valuable for the anorectic for many reasons. Therapy is an environment for exploration, digestion and the ultimate release of the complex of feelings—appalling despair, disgust, upset, sadness about what one has "done to oneself." The presence of a genuinely sympathetic therapist makes it possible for the woman to regard her experiences in a new light. This stance on the part of the therapist cannot be willed, it arises organically from the prescriptive measures I have suggested. It depends upon the therapist relating to the actual person engaged in the anorectic behavior. This respect can be conveyed in an authentic manner so that the anorectic can see herself from the outside, with the eyes of the therapist. She can confront the reality of what she is and has been doing to herself. She can do this because she feels the therapist's respect. She has a therapeutic partner who in failing to reject her as she rejects herself, causes her to look at herself in a new light.

The open acknowledgment that the anorectic is in charge of her own food supply recognizes that she has things to learn about food and is capable of learning them *from the inside* and *for herself*. For years she has been living with a self-imposed scheme of one kind or another. Her food has not been about matching her hunger and pleasing her appetite but about overriding it, together with other feelings that arise in her. She is now being given the opportunity to learn to have food as part of her life, as a sustaining, enjoyable feature of it. But we are getting ahead of the story here, for before food can become a positive experience there will be many painful struggles to overcome on the way. Suffice it to say now that an important area for discussion in the initial period of the therapy relationship will be the development of an understanding of the food refusal. This understanding rests on an acceptance of what is, not on its denial or negation.

In addition, such acceptance makes theoretical sense. The development of anorexia is in part fueled by the need to impose some stability and control on a chaotic and unintegrated internal life. The control over food intake is an attempt to ameliorate the inability to control emotional incursions. The anorectic seeks to control her physical desires and needs—her appetites—and in so doing gains a measure of self-respect. Her emotional appetites and the restraints she exercises on them will in time come to be understood in the same way.

As I have already discussed, emotional desire is an extremely fraught and complex area for women. Although paradoxically the culture has invested women with responsibility for the understanding of and response to the emotional needs of others, women's facility to recognize and meet their *own* needs is restricted by developmental imperatives that create taboos on a whole range of self-expression. The anorectic woman has not experienced, in her development, an ease with recognizing her emotional needs. In woman after woman I have observed a pattern in which needs and initiations are ignored, disparaged or thwarted in some way. This has enormous implications for the themes that will be worked through in the therapy, but a precondition for cutting into the notion that one's desires are bad or wrong is the arrangement made with the woman in relation to her control over her food. If she can be sure that you will allow her to act on her own wishes as far as food goes (however circumscribed they doubtless are at this stage), slowly and gradually the therapist is kindling the idea that desire and implementation are not in themselves bad.

Beyond this theoretical point is the tremendously positive effect such an arrangement has in creating a therapeutic working alliance. For vast periods of the therapy, the therapist will be relying on just such an alliance to help the woman grope her way out of the most persistent vicissitudes of the anorectic defense structure. The woman relies on her experience of the therapist as someone who is genuinely supportive and reasonable. The arrangement with food exemplifies this stance perfectly. Of course, this is not to ignore by any means the woman's food intake or her weight. The therapist needs to keep an awareness about these matters and especially to make openings in the therapy to let the client talk freely about food.

It will be obvious from what I am saying that the restoration of weight is not a primary goal of treatment in the early stages. Indeed this is stated to the client and to those family members whose involvement with her has intensely revolved around encouraging her to eat and put on weight. This may be disheartening news for the family who come seeking help, hoping that I will be able to "get the person to eat." However, I have discovered that they are (albeit with some difficulty) able to understand that this emphasis could short-circuit any long-term recovery as it fails to come to grips with the food refusal in the first place or to help the person develop an inner confidence about putting food back into her life positively. Weight gain is not a useful primary goal, then, even though it would be desirable from the point of view of decreasing the anxiety of those around the anorectic woman.

In addition it is of course true that severe starvation brings in its wake problems which impede the recovery process itself. Starvation creates particular thought processes—not simply the preoccupation with food[1] but also emotional states which career from depression to mania. However, since taking over the feeding of the woman rarely achieves long-term results that are satisfactory, the benefits in not introducing such a regimen outweigh the disadvantages. It has been gratifying for women I have worked with to recognize that their energy level and their cognitive ability are affected by what they eat or do not eat, and to discover that food does have a function as a fuel for the body apart from the symbolic functions with which it is invested. It places food in a perspective they had failed to see, and such experiences felt from the inside are often singularly empowering.

Many practitioners may perhaps object to the notion that the woman who is so clearly unable to eat properly should be allowed to continue to exercise control over her eating. They see the non-eating as a severe threat to her mental and physical well-being and take as their priority the restoration of weight to its pre-anorectic level. Therapeutic work either goes hand in hand with this or follows the attainment of goal.[2] While I sympathize with the desire to help the woman towards gaining strength rapidly, and certainly understand the pressure the practitioner feels when she or he is confronted with the figure of an emaciated person who is withdrawn, sullen and weak, I think that such an emphasis misses key dimensions of therapeutic work which will be essential in the recovery. Recovery does not rest on the reversing of the food refusal and restoring weight loss. Weight gain under such circumstances can often not be maintained, rendering in the client yet more desperate feelings about her inability to achieve "success" in any other sphere apart from weight loss.

Recovery needs to include investigation and a working through of the painful states that the anorexia blanketed. In other words, what is required is a psychic restructuring, so that the conditions that made the woman ripe for anorexia no longer obtain.

By allowing the processes of learning to eat again and put on weight to remain firmly within the province of the client, the therapeutic partnership can begin the task of understanding the meaning of the food refusal for the individual woman. In general, as we have seen, these meanings will reflect negative aspects of the woman's self-concept. The avoidance of food is consciously tied to a desire to lose weight. Such an action is felt as a way to become more acceptable and more attractive. At the same time, for many women, an account receivable and account payable system operates. If they give up one thing—eating— they can at least eke out a theoretical entitlement to some- thing else. This is often how the food refusal is conceived of in its early stages. Soon enough, however, the account receivable is never collected. The amount to be paid grows, making a withdrawal too costly. Now the meaning shifts. The refusal to respond to hunger by eating becomes the proof that these women are successfully denying them- selves and in so doing ensuring some psychic return. Investigating such ideas in detail brings up the unconscious motivations and compromises that result in not eating. We discover that alongside the hunger for food a deep hunger for life lies thwarted and bound up in the food refusal. This refusal is a compromise position, a way to deal with problematic themes in the woman's life. When we explore the content of these themes further we are struck by how powerfully the themes of initiation, autonomy, nurturance and dependency—so important in a woman's psychology today—are embedded in the imagined gains from the food refusal. As we have seen, taboos about self-actualization and needs are structured into each woman's psyche. Negotiating the desire to initiate and the desire for nurture are key features in the development of a feminine psychology.[3] A girl grows up learning to turn her own needs into the servicing of needs in others. She becomes accustomed to restricting her initiatives to those areas that are a response to others' declared needs. As a result she loses touch with her own needs so that they become not only repressed but unrecognized and undeveloped. More damaging, perhaps, she takes on the idea that needs that do arise from within her are somehow wrong, and that she herself is all wrong for having them.

The food refusal can be seen to be a graphic gagging of desire, a block on having what is so wanted. It becomes a model for deprivation in all areas. "If I can successfully deny myself food, I will be able to crush the other desires that arise in me." The determination associated with the refusal of food is much more than the expression of will, it is an example of the brake on desire in general that exists in the woman. It is a measure of perceived restriction in other areas of self-expression. "I'm not permitted to do this which I want to do."

The woman with anorexia has uncannily strong opinions. Her socialization process has been *less* rather than more congruent with the culture at large. Even if she has appeared on the surface to have been reasonably contented, she has not in actuality been able to accept the strictures and constraints of her role. She has balked at them inside. She has not been able to suppress her feelings successfully and yet she has had no validation for them. She ends up with a character that contains determination and anger as a result. She feels enormously guilty at the fact of her desires. She may not be able to articulate them fully but she experiences their force. They feel uncontrollable. She may feel chaotic inside, at the mercy of tumultuous emotions. She wants to burst out, to smash things, to have all the goods in the shops, all the experiences life has to offer, but at the same time she will have none of them. Desire is curtailed and she proves to herself repeatedly that these inconvenient and encumbering needs that so plague and disturb her can be managed and denied. The agonizing process of suppressing such powerful and conflicting feelings requires a tremendous and ever-increasing vigilance. As they threaten to erupt, so she must crush them more vehemently. The more a want is felt, the more stringent will be the food refusal. One and one makes two. The logic of parallel denial shapes her thinking and actions.

Many women are only able to manage such insistent deprivation by the simultaneous explosions of uncontrollable desire expressed in binging on large quantities of food. The first binge can be an extremely disheartening experience for the woman whose whole energy has been put into establishing and maintaining control over herself. It can seem to undermine her entire achievement and even her raison d'être. It feels humiliating and the woman is forced to confront the underbelly of her capacity to deny herself. She feels subject to that very monstrous desire she has tried to contain. It sweeps her up and sends her through pounds and pounds of food in a very short space of time. Just as the denial creates a temporary relief by proving that want can be overcome, so the binge explodes that myth and reveals the neediness and desperation that refuse to be bound up.

As the therapist and anorectic woman explore together the meaning of the binge, and live through the details of it, they come to grips with the consequences of the deprivation as well as the intensity of wanting manifest in the binge. The binge is the relief, the letting go, the taking in, the attempted meeting of desire. With the submission to the binge (which is how it feels) the woman is taken over by the unruly and desperately hungry part of herself, the part that she suppresses most of the time. Her wanting and wanton part is in ascendancy. As she ferrets around stuffing one food after another into her mouth, she is looking for a way to assuage an unleashed appetite. She goes from food to food looking for the one that will satisfy her, quiet the roaring inside her, meet a hunger that cannot be met by food. Like the little baby wailing for its feed who experiences extreme discomfort and has, as yet, no sense of continuity, no sense that the next moment will bring relief, the binging woman is feverishly out of contact with all but her desperate need and a kind of indistinct knowledge of the impossibility of meeting her need for soothing. She finds herself temporarily in a time and emotional capsule, divorced from all but the most basic and insistent urges towards comfort. She is cut off from contact with others and from her environment in general. Her anorectic withdrawal seals her in one bubble, her frenetic binging in another equally impenetrable one. The search she is on is essentially autistic, the environment is useless—worse, even, it is hopeless and dangerous to try to meet needs through contact. Better to stuff them down again with food, stop up the wanting, quiet the monster inside.

But, alas, this search for a comfort that cannot be found serves to increase the anorectic woman's sense of self-hatred. She breaks out of her cell and the recriminations pour forth. She castigates herself for greed, stupidity, the ridiculousness of her endeavor. She must now deal with the consequences of having let go.

In therapy we explore the act of submission to the binge. We identify the feelings that propelled it and the feelings manifest in it at every stage. We slow down the action and play it through frame by frame. We break the autistic hold on those moments and try to decipher the wanting, the searching, the desperateness. We try to provide an under-

standing that in its accuracy will effectively counterpose
the self-disgust and rejection that has inevitably ensued. In
honoring the symptom we learn something of what it is
meant to do. But we must go beyond simply understanding
and provide a compassionate attitude towards the break-
out. We can see it as not simply the opposite of repression,
but the thwarted desire to go towards the environment.
Food, nourishment, first given by the mother, is the most
profound expression of relationship—the symbol for entry
into the world. It *is* the world for the first few months of
life—the mode of communication between mother and
child—and it prepares one for the assumption of life outside the dyad. The binge then expresses the desire to break
out of the primary autism into the dyad and then the world,
but at the same time it acts as a stranglehold preventing
that very engagement.

To decipher meaning is to empower, to give a purpose
to what appears at first to be a solely self-destructive act.
To recognize the thrust towards life that is implicit in the
binge is to begin to provide options for alternative ways to
construe and act on that desire. By this I do not mean that
intervention is possible at a purely cognitive level. Rather,
reliving with another the intimate details of a binge and the
feelings contained in it, gives back that experience (that
the binge signified) to the person herself. She is less able
to split it off, to hide away her desire. She has an opportunity to see and experience with another its strength and to
notice the determination of her struggle to squash it. Such
realizations necessarily confront the anorectic solution to
needs. They foster a recognition of the fallacious account-
ing system the woman has been relying upon. By reliving
such an experience with another who refuses the punitive,
judging role, the most precious ideas attached to the having and suppression of needs are challenged.

Beyond the binge lies the purge of one kind or another:

the attempted cleansing-out operation after the food blitz. All that has been ingested needs to be done away with. Food and "fat"—the evidence of need (and met need at that)—must be extinguished. Again, exploration of the purge within the therapy relationship renders its details alive. If the binge is an attempt at getting, a search for soothing, then the purge contains within it the repudiation of the need and tangible evidence that such soothing cannot be digested. The soothing so feverishly pursued in the binge has eluded the anorectic. It now propels her with equal force towards elimination. Soothing cannot emanate from taking in but from expulsion. The purge brings a relief. It puts one back to square one. The disturbance is quelled. The internal shock troops that police the needs have performed on cue. The circle turns. The reexperiencing of the details of the binge and purge within the therapy relationship reveal at a visceral level the internal war inside the woman.

We can see how the exploration of the symbolic and actual meanings of the food refusal goes a long way towards the demystification of the symptom. The understandings that can be gained in a therapeutic relationship do not come easily or without resistance. There will be resistance to both the understandings that have to be grappled with and the changes that need to occur in the actual food intake. Of course this is obvious once one takes seriously the anorexia itself, for this way of being is not one that has been "chosen," but the psychological solution for a set of internal problems. Problems that can fade away in a flash of insight do not require solutions as dramatic as anorexia.

The anorexic position is a highly tenacious one because it holds in check the frail false self created to keep in the hated needs and to defend the as-yet-undeveloped self. Thus anticipating rapid change both in self-image or in eating behavior is unrealistic. Similarly, a linear progression is extremely unlikely. The therapy will probably proceed by fits and starts. The therapist needs to hold to the experience of continuity that the client cannot yet feel. The eureka type of understandings, that seem to promise so much hope in the moment, will be forgotten and need to be gone over again and again. Each eating experience that seems to start in motion a new, more organic way of being with food, will be undone a number of times by the reinstituting of denial or the reoccurrence of binging. The patience to live through these difficulties, the very ones that the client finds so out of reach, is the hallmark of competent therapy. Almost nothing can be achieved in a partnership in which the therapist cannot tolerate the agonies that are central to the process. The discouragement the therapist feels in her or himself when a setback occurs is insignificant when compared to the anguish that is infusing the client. The client's anguish must be given direct expression without the "setback" being seen as a failure. The blocking of understanding, or the return to ritualistic behaviors, is simply part of the process of working through the anorexia. It will be months and months, more likely several years, before the anorectic woman has an experience of continuity in relation to being able to eat, or in feeling confident that the range of feelings that arise in her are acceptable.

In my experience, few anorectic women are able to alter their eating behavior radically in the first phase of therapy. Of course those practitioners involved in food management see changes in eating patterns early on in the course of treatment, but frequently, I fear, the women are still left with a phobic relation to food and an inability to build a structure that can guide them from the inside. Many women who have gone through such a treatment program express the fear that they will not be able to

limit their eating when they break out of the rigidity of the
new scheme that substitutes for their previously self-imposed
controls. Although weight gain and menstrual functions
are achieved, the fear of food and of fatness continues to
plague the woman. The goal of the approach outlined here
is to enable the woman to have the best possible chance of
living her life *unafraid* of food. The aim is to help her
develop the necessary skills to respond to her body's desires for an unlimited range of foodstuffs. We are helping
her to begin to feel comfortable with hunger signals so that
she can respond judicially and without alarm, and feel
confident that she can stop eating when physically satisfied.

Although this is a goal of successful therapeutic work,
there is no sense in which it is wise to anticipate that the
woman will be able to experiment freely enough with food
to achieve this until well into the therapy. Except in atypi-
cal cases—which, of course, one is bound to come across—
the strategy employed by the therapist is to shift the emphasis
away from the achievement of such a goal into two areas.
One is the exploration of the *experience* of food on a daily
basis, and the second, the investigation of those themes
which led initially to the onset of the symptom and those
issues which are live in keeping the symptom going. Unless the conflicts, despairs and myriad themes enmeshed in
the anorexia become disentangled and are directly confronted, the defense will persist or there will be a symptom
switch.[4]

It would also be unwise to anticipate that the first time
the woman is able to break out of the rigid pattern in
relation to food she will have a good eating experience.
Much remorse may be felt for what is experienced as a
giving up of control. Rather than the event being a straightforwardly positive one, it will be laced with anguish and
worry. It will be important to anticipate the psychic difficulties that such an event may produce. Progress, from the

practitioner's point of view, does not necessarily appear as achievement to the client. It will be at best an ambivalent experience. Being able to hold in one's emotional vocabulary both the positive and anxiety-provoking experiences provides a therapeutic service to the woman who is not yet able to contain such contradictory feelings for herself with ease.

It will also be important for the therapist to be especially careful about setting up expectations of what the woman should be able to achieve at any particular point in terms of specific food intake, or attitude towards food. A woman whose personality contains the capacity to please others, and to be so apparently accommodating, runs the risk of using a food experience deemed to be an experiment in growth as a transferential attempt to please the therapist. The "gift" of eating that the woman gives the therapist in such circumstances is simply that and not the expression of the resolution of her difficulties. Indeed it may well bode badly for eventual recovery in which the eating experience must come from an *inner* confidence that it is all right to eat. (Paradoxically, in this way, the recovered anorectic may have something few other woman have—a wholesome entitlement to the food women are encouraged to deny themselves in one way or another.) The therapist's job is to provide the confidence that eating might turn out to be a positive activity at some point. Of course, the client will be nervous and only half-believe that she can eat and get out of the anorexia. The therapist provides the confidence that so far eludes the woman. It will be important to convey the idea that each eating experience is an opportunity for experimentation rather than a signal of success or failure. In this way each eating experience can be examined and its emotional and physical resonances evaluated.

# NOTES

1. It does this in "normal" starving people too. Keys, A., Brozek, J., Herschel, A., Mickelson, O. and Taylor, H.L., *The Biology of Human Starvation*, vol. 1 (Minneapolis, University of Minnesota Press, 1950).

2. See for example: Crisp, A.H., *Let Me Be* (London and New York, 1980); Bruch, H., *Eating Disorders; Obesity, Anorexia Nervosa and the Person Within* (New York, 1973); Palmer, R.L., *Anorexia Nervosa* (London, 1980); Dally, P., *Anorexia Nervosa* (London, 1969); Minuchin, S., Rosman, B.L. and Baker, L., *Psychosomatic Families: Anorexia Nervosa in Context* (Cambridge, Mass., 1978).

3. Eichenbaum, L. and Orbach, S., *What Do Women Want?* (London and New York, 1983); Eichenbaum, L. and Orbach, S., *Understanding Women* (New York, 1983).

4. Unfortunately, my colleagues and I have come across many instances of symptom switching from alcoholism to bulimia, from anorexia to heroin addiction and from eating problems to phobic responses.

# 9 Focusing on the Body: The Corporeal Sense of Self

Untangling the meanings of the food refusal and helping the individual woman to develop a new and positive relationship to eating goes hand in hand with the exploration of ideas the woman has about her body-image. Consciously, the food refusal was first instigated as a way to cope with discomfort in her body. Commonly the unease arose from bodily desires she felt, her disgust at "the fat," or the appearance of her first period before she was prepared for it, and so on. Obviously such issues are very important and will need to be taken up in the therapy in the process of helping her to eat again. But the resistance to engaging again in so-called normal eating behavior is often subsumed by the twin fears of weight gain and "going out of control." These two fears exemplify the anorectic woman's relationship with her body. The body is experienced as an object that must be controlled or it will control. The emaciated body demonstrates that *she* controls her body whereas the average-sized body controls *her*. There are but two options.

There is no notion or sense of the body as an integrated aspect of self, rather it represents in physical form the internal struggles to control needs and unsatisfactory object

187

relations, an attempt to dress oneself with an acceptable self-image. The body is something one puts on and takes off, not the place in which one lives. In this stance towards her body the anorectic woman is, as we have already noted, exaggerating the response that all women in this culture come to have towards their bodies. But the fact that it is such an exaggerated response leads us back to a consideration of the developmental issues crucial in the acquisition of a corporeal sense of self and to their unfolding in the therapeutic process.

The anorectic woman appears to show enormous receptivity to culturally sanctioned messages about physical femininity. This receptivity is built on her shaky corporeal sense of herself. As we have seen, her psychosomatic development as a whole has doubtless been stunted. Just as we saw that the construction of femininity creates in women's psychology in general a feeling of insecurity, a defense against the expression of dependency or autonomy and a sense that needs and initiations will neither be fully met nor approved of, so women's psychology includes a discomfort to some extent or another with the body in which they live.

The starkness with which the extreme form of this discomfort is expressed by the woman with anorexia is in her physical appearance. To the onlooker her appearance is ghastly, but the anorectic woman herself does not see this. The alienated body is simply something to be dealt with. The struggle to make it smaller and ever smaller is a means of placing the body under her control. It can never be quite small enough to be safely controlled rather than controlling.

For discussions about body size to be useful to the anorectic woman they must therefore take into account this important meaning, otherwise an attempted dialogue about the body misfires into tragic misunderstanding. It is no

good challenging this view of the body in the first instance
for it is the meaning with which it has become invested.
Just as avoiding tussles over food intake provides the
preconditions that eating can once again (or for the first
time) enter the woman's world as a positive experience, so
respecting the meaning of the body and taking that meaning into account establishes the preconditions for a recon-
sideration of the body.

The client here is a twenty-six-year-old, white, single,
professional woman. She stands 5 feet 2 inches (1.55m),
weighs 90 lbs. (40.9kg), has been symptomatic for seven
years. The lowest weight she was seen at was 80 lbs.
(36.3kg).

CLIENT: If I were to be 105 lbs. (47.7kg), I would just feel
     so scared.
THERAPIST: In what sense would you feel scared?
CLIENT: I'd be so ugly, fat, all exposed . . . I would be
     obliterated . . . my body would have taken over.
THERAPIST: It seems as though your "body" has taken on
     some particular meanings, then?
CLIENT: Yes. It is like my ability to control my needs has
     vanished and I would be at the mercy of them again.
     When I am this size, I just about feel in charge. At
     least I'm not vulnerable, weepy and all over the show
     in the way I was when I was FAT—well, 105 lbs. . . .
     I know that isn't really fat, but it is on the border, and
     even at that size I felt exposed and horrible.

With this meaning firmly established between client and
therapist, it is then possible to examine the other nuances
related to body-image and the meanings ascribed to them.
The anorectic's internal logic has been understood and
related to, thus freeing her to consider other things she
might be trying to express through her body. In this in-

stance, acceptance of the anorectic's view meant that the therapist was able to speak to that aspect of the client that had some inkling that indeed 105 lbs. was hardly fat. This made it possible for the dialogue to proceed.

THERAPIST: It seems that somewhere, you have a sense that 105 lbs. is not actually fat.

CLIENT: Well, objectively I suppose it isn't. But I don't think I could face being that big again.

THERAPIST: I think we understand some of why that is, not all of it by any means, but while we are working together on getting a more complete understanding, it is useful for us to have this other sense of 105 lbs. acknowledged between us.

In this way, without forcing an unacceptable idea on the client, the therapist is raising "reality" issues about size and weight. She is developing a treatment alliance with the part of the woman which has an interest in "getting better" and being a more normal size. Maintaining a dialogue with this aspect of the woman is only possible because the distortions (that is to say, the meanings that the woman carries around about the emaciated body she favors) are accepted and understood.

The therapeutic process will throw up a tremendous amount of material related to the body. This cannot be strictly understood in terms of body-image because an important way in which the woman talks about her body is her wish to do away with it or exist without a body at all. The body has come to represent the existence and insistence of needs. The doing away with the body, then, is an attempted solution to the unpredictable appearance of need. I think it is in this sense that Gull,[1] the Victorian physician who first named the syndrome of anorexia nervosa in English, saw it as a morbid disease. The sense one has of the woman projecting her self-hatred on to her body seems at first glance morbid. Deeper examination does not reveal morbidity as such, but the importance of examining the *wish* to be without or do away with the body. In trying to cope with her self-hatred, she takes as her task the creation of a new person. We have seen how through denial and the repression of needs she makes out of herself a persona that she finds more acceptable. She measures her success in this task by her diminishing size. The emaciated body is the tangible evidence she uses to reassure herself that she has indeed done away with the unacceptable self. She sees her diminutive presence as the visible expression of this. Thus much discussion in the therapy will center on the theme of self-hatred and the subsequent attempted transformation of self that the woman has initiated, rather than a strict emphasis on the topic of the body, which provided the impetus for the dialogue.

In direct relation to her body, however, the woman with anorexia often thinks that her body and its functions have appeared to be "out of control" during a particularly difficult time in her life. This coincidence of experiences then predisposes the woman to take up some kind of difficulty around food or body-image. The resulting anorexia, and the wish to do away with the body, are in these instances more about the dreaded experiences of being out of control than strictly about the suppression of need. For example, as we have seen (page 71), Jean first menstruated when she was eleven. She was unprepared for the event and when she told her mother about the fact that she was bleeding, she was greeted with a mixture of disbelief and alarm. Her mother, equally unprepared for an extremely early appearance of the menarche, was unable to respond in a way that imbued the event with the required positiveness. Jean, feeling quite odd, came to feel ashamed of this thing that was happening to her that she neither understood nor had expected. She did not have the emotional vocabularly to cope with the event. She was essentially alone in the experience, with no resources to draw on. The loss of control and the fear and upset she felt were projected on to her body, which became "out of control." The nurse at school explained to her that she started her period so early because she was a "big girl." She resolved to become a smaller one and made sure that her period did not reappear for thirteen more years.

Similarly, Audrey felt she could not stop herself pursuing physical sensations as a teenager. She smoked a lot of pot, felt driven to eat large quantities of food, and felt herself to be so much at the mercy of her sexual urges that she was getting into complicated emotional tangles with too many people. She described her problems to herself as "my body going off full steam without me," feeling led by its urges and very out of control. For both these women, the anorexia brought short-term relief in the active experience of controlling their bodies. As a result, they felt less vulnerable to the body's demands. Neither could grasp or use the notion that one could negotiate between being controlled or controlling. Either option was inharmonious, but the latter measurably so.

An important aspect of the therapeutic work centers on the creation of conditions in which the halted developmental steps needed for the acquisition of a psychosomatic unity can be resumed. Much therapeutic effort will be expended in that direction, for the ability to *experience* the body as the place one lives in is central to the recovery from anorexia. The body needs to be transformed from being experienced as an object—alienated and despised—to an expression of self. This is a thorny idea to convey, as in a curious way, the anorectic while apparently rejecting her body is simultaneously insisting that others relate to her through her body. In other words it has become a form of expression for her. However, it is an expressiveness born of defense rather than deriving from an internal sense of well-being. Thus the distortion or the difficulty is not crucially at the level of *idea* but at the level of psychosomatic unrelatedness.[2]

The process towards de-alienation and satisfactory corporization[3] occurs in the therapy relationship in several ways. In the first place this is realized through the body becoming the subject of conversation. By entering into a dialogue about the meaning of the body, the experience of body alienation, the use of the body as an object, the "perfected" body as a means to a new persona, and the projections on to the body, those very meanings are examined, understood, and then in turn transformed. By scrutinizing her relation to the body the anorectic is activating a new mode of being in and with it. The therapist, in sharing that experience with her, is aiding the process of corporization.

Unraveling these meanings is a complex process and one which needs to take account of the culture's fetishism with the female body. Each woman has a difficult struggle before her. Firstly she is working towards experiencing her body as the place in which she lives. At the same time she has to find a way of reconciling the body as owned and lived in with the opposing cultural thrust of the female body as object. The particular form of alienation exemplified in our culture at once objectifies social relations through commoditization, while offering "rehumanization" through the vehicle of the female body and female sexuality. Each woman carries within her the experiential knowledge of cultural practices. The anorectic woman has been both expressing and rejecting this cultural practice, in an exaggerated way. Her diminutive, essentially prepubescent body exemplifies the limited space a woman feels entitled to take up. At the same time, by desexualizing herself through diminishing her hips and breasts, and banishing her periods, she is denying essential aspects of adult femininity. Looking like a girl/boy she defies simple definition and thus control. As she comes out of the anorexia and works on developing a comfort in and with her body she is negotiating a new and possibly hostile territory, for there are few images of adult femininity that are not appropriated or objectified by the culture. To the extent to which she is able to reject the cultural laws she may feel isolated and on untested ground. She may experience a new precariousness within her body, one that emanates from consciously breaking with the cultural forms she had previously been attempting to follow. The way forward is untested and unknown and as such presents its own difficulties.

But beyond the manifest content about the body is the therapeutic relationship which in speaking to the undeveloped self allows the nascent psychosomatic self to continue to grow. The therapist is relating to an undeveloped embryonic self[4] which has remained strangled behind a defense structure. The "false self" of ordinary social intercourse is not the point of contact in the therapy relationship. Instead, it is the task of the therapist to make a relationship with the vulnerable undeveloped self so that it can continue through its developmental paces. By being in tune with that developing self it becomes possible for the woman to move past the developmental lesions which have created such a chasm between the embryonic self on the one hand and the "false self" and the "false body" on the other.

This is not by any means to leave aside body size *per se* as an area for discussion. It simply alerts those working with anorectics to the extra dimensions to be considered. If these are not taken into account possible areas of misunderstanding and avoidable stumbling blocks to productive work can arise when talking about the body. It will be

quite proper and necessary to take up in an extremely
detailed way what different sizes and weights actually have
meant for the individual woman. Frequently we learn that
fat (by which is meant anything bigger than thin) is linked
with sloth, indulgence, greed and unhappiness. Presented
with such strong images one might be tempted not to
pursue the matter further but to work hard to disassociate
such ideas from the objective size. However, in my experience, looking at these meanings and the times at which the
client was, or felt herself to be, fat reveals a much more
complex picture that she carries around with her. We
discover times when "fat" was not only associated with
unhappiness and sloth but with a kind of contentment.

Fat may have been the state the client was in only
retrospectively. For example, she might have been at quite
a "normal" size when she broke up with her husband, or
started to menstruate, or had an abortion. This experience
sent shock waves through her system and she then tried to
right the wrong by changing herself in some fundamental
way. This was translated into changing her body. Through
the development of anorexia, that original body size then
comes to be redrawn and remembered as fat although she
was not in fact fat, and the marriage certainly did not
dissolve because of her size, her adolescent crises were not
marked by weight gain or loss, nor was the pregnancy the
result of being large! For many women, especially those
whose anorexia followed actual periods of being larger
than average (as opposed to imagining oneself as fat),
fatness may in fact have quite positive connotations. These
associations may be deeply buried under the more conventional response of disgust, but it is important to discover
them. As long as they remain uninvestigated they represent
a threat to the anorectic woman and make it hard for her to
conceive of being a size that is neither fat nor thin. They

become a magnet pulling her out of thinness and into fatness.

What is required in the process of working through the anorectic stance is a coming to terms with the emotional nuances and images associated with a whole range of body sizes. In addition, talking through what fat actually meant and the limited ideas the anorectic woman has associated with it more recently, restores to her a much richer palate of meanings. These meanings are ones that she will eventually be able to draw upon during the process of recovery. Reaching 100 lbs. (45.45kg), for example, will not be a purely dreaded experience, for she will have reintegrated the positive experience (or at the very least not only be focused on the negative experiences and values) with that weight. Thus we can see the advantages and necessity of a thorough investigation of how the individual woman felt in relation to various weights. There is otherwise the possibility that the therapist will collude with the woman's tendency to conflate her experiences into one, and come up with a singularly negative rather than a complex picture of fat and thin. Having said this, it is important to bear in mind that becoming bigger will, to some extent, be a difficult experience for the woman. However much part of her may be ready for growth and may even greet the reappearance of menstruation and curves—in short a woman's healthy body—another part of her is losing a known way of being. Psychological growth contains a poignancy even when it is exhilarating.

Clothes and the trying on of various images that clothing reflect are important in this context. Many anorectic women do not feel entitled to dress to please themselves. Consciously choosing clothing that will attract attention to oneself, wearing bright colors or clothes that fit, or choosing clothing at all is regarded as indulgent. Dress makes a statement about a want. Often clothing is used to hide a very skinny body from the world. The woman's diminutive size has started to cause frequent enough comments for her to feel uncomfortable and to fear that others will be able to get to her body by their comments. She covers up her stick-like arms and legs, wears several layers of clothing and keeps close inside her the knowledge of how very small she is. She is soothed by her ability apparently to hide her secret achievement of smallness from others. But clothes of course are no simple matter in our culture or in the mind of the anorectic woman. They convey all manner of meanings, just as the way the wearer carries herself gives clues to how she feels and is part of an overall image she projects. Like so many other aspects of body language, clothes and dressing are fraught with tension and pain for the anorectic woman. Her desire to be attractive by doing away with her body or making it smaller, has not resulted in a degree of comfort but merely changed the focus of discomfort. It is indeed hard to dress a very skinny body in a way that is appealing. We are simply not used to seeing clothes that hang on a rail-like body as aesthetically pleasing. In addition, many women who suffer from anorexia find it hard to buy clothes for themselves. The ordeal of going shopping and engendering the comments of others in the changing room, while finding few things that fit, is difficult.

In addition, many women find it extremely hard to spend money on themselves. It is another facet of denial and deprivation. Almost all sums of money will seem quite large and be associated with overindulgence. Again we see the evidence of the taboo against recognizing and meeting a need. Money not spent is proof of the ability to eliminate need. Further, close examination of the block on spending often reveals a particular symbolic meaning attached to money. Women who, prior to the onset of anorexia, felt relatively free with money now find themselves reluctant to spend. Giving it up is felt as a depletion and a gargantuan indulgence. One is not felt to be worth that much. One does not deserve a dress/bag/shoes/theater ticket, etc. The subsequent hoarding then becomes justified as a desperate attempt at some kind of security. Money saved is associated with being "good," and protection against future need. Dire circumstances are around the corner and money must be conserved for such occasions. Just as not eating acts as an insurance policy against what might happen, so by not spending money now the security that is missing in the present can be assured in the future. "I don't want to be poor and miserable when I am older" is a frequent justification of this way of coping with money. Being frugal and miserable now is more acceptable. This sentiment of course echoes the feeling that the environment will never be benevolent. What one has at present is the maximum possible happiness, wealth, etc., even if plainly the person is hardly contented.

Alongside a detailed examination of the varied meanings of fat, thin and normal there may be some need to focus attention on how the anorectic woman lives in and with her body at the various weights. As with all themes that are important in the lives of anorectics, close attention to the nuances of feeling expressed around body-image and exploration of the disgust that so many women feel toward their bodies, is of paramount importance. Towards the end phase of therapy, as the woman is able to eat more and her body is gradually transforming, the therapist makes herself available to work through the feelings that being "normal" engender. The woman may fear that if she looks "normal" she may have to do whatever is included in her definition of what "normal" women do. An important component of the therapy will be for her to find ways to express herself in alternative ways other than through the dramatic transformation of her body. If feeling lousy, she needs to find a response to compliments about how well she looks such as "But actually I'm not feeling so good in myself today" or "Yes, it's curious, my food and body problems are mostly cleared up but I can still feel very blue" and so on. In other words she needs a richer vocabulary for self-expression than a diminishing body and a diminishing food intake. She has to learn to voice her feelings more directly.

Understanding how any particular woman feels about her body during the active anorectic phase is important too. A diminutive size does not always represent a retiring presence. Surprisingly, perhaps, the woman may project a comfort in her body even if the onlooker finds that disconcerting. She may not take up the stance traditionally associated with anorexia, i.e. the withered, retreating, bulging-eyed frail figure. She may appreciate the strength that her physical workouts have given her and she may display her arm muscles nonchalantly. Many an anorectic model is paid handsomely to display clothes on her body, and many an anorectic dancer performs in public. In fact she may contemplate such displays of the body only because it is felt to be skinny enough. The putting on of weight is then experienced as removing the possibility to display oneself or perform.

Many women do, of course, feel so uncomfortable in their tiny bodies that they shroud them in an attempt at concealment. This discomfort may or may not relate simply to the current size. The woman may, for example, have hidden her body or sat uncomfortably in it when she was at a size perfectly within the norm. The therapy relationship provides the context for looking at the various adaptations she has made. An important proviso is the therapist's ability to project a comfort with *her* body. This will be extremely reassuring to the client and it will enable her to work towards having a body that she too can be at ease with. A therapist whose body changes size during the therapy relationship can be extremely disconcerting and confusing to the client. A degree of comfort with one's body, which means an acceptance of its size and an ability to project this, is a preliminary condition for doing therapy with the anorectic woman. In fact the difficulties for the client in the area of the body are so acute that (except for the biologically necessitated changes of pregnancy) therapists whose bodies go up and down in size would find it quite hard to sort out the communications about the body in the therapy relationship. Having said this, it does not imply that the client will regard the therapist's body as a constant; the ways she sees it will be of enormous importance in the therapy relationship and hence in the working through of the distortions the client has towards her own body.

This was vividly illustrated in my work when I took a summer break and asked my clients who required coverage during that period if they had any preferences as to who they might see during my absence. Their replies were extremely interesting as they included references to this very point: "I don't want to see anyone who is dieting"; "I would like to see someone who has some knowledge of anorexia. If it is personal knowledge of this problem I want it to be in the past," and so on. In discussing their wishes we discovered how very important to them was the perception of me as not having an eating/weight problem. Precisely because they projected a sureness about my food supplies and comfort with my body on to me, they could use that confidence to work through these very problematic issues themselves. The discussions we had could take in their painfully envious feelings, their wonder at how anyone could achieve such ease and so on.

At times during the therapy, the therapist's body was seen to grow, to take up enormous space in the therapy room and to be almost menacing. The fact that the therapist's body had not in fact changed size was extremely useful in helping the client work through what was being projected on to the body of the therapist. In this example, the therapist's body had taken on characteristics the client associated with her own despised body. It seemed large, clumsy and to be secreting needs. An examination of the details of this experience revealed the bad object relations the body symbolizes. The therapist's body appeared as the tantalizing mother who would not satisfy the child's need. The imagined "fat" exposed both need and the possibility of fulfillment. The vision was excruciating for the client who, living with a history of unmet needs, could not bear the visibility of either projection. The full force of this conflict was experienced within the therapy relationship, and the client, able to grasp the distortion on to the therapist's body, was able to use this experience to find a new way to be in her own body.

Needs unsatisfied are the most difficult of issues to work through for the anorectic woman. The appearance of a need is felt to be so threatening that it is generally repressed or transmuted into a more negotiable form. A critical issue to be grappled with, and worked through, in therapy is the fact and consequences of the mismatching of historic needs. This mismatching has resulted in feelings of unworthiness which make it hard for the woman to feel capable or entitled to meet needs that come up in the present. If needs are consistently not met early on in life, or if there is no usable explanation as to why needs go unmet, there are two serious consequences. Firstly, the developing person takes into her or himself the idea that needs in themselves are bad. At the same time he or she does not develop the facility to deal with needs as they spontaneously arise except with alarm or repression.

It is startling for the anorectic woman to realize that new

needs are produced on a daily, even hourly basis and that life cannot easily proceed with continual strategies to avoid them. Small needs and big needs, meetable needs and unmeetable needs seems to have become inseparable in the anorectic's mind and value system. Wanting a piece of chocolate, wanting to make a friend, wanting to sleep, wanting to become a concert pianist, wanting to wear bright clothes are all equally taboo and impossible to meet. Any need could be unmeetable, therefore all needs should be avoided. The therapy has to face this confusion around needs squarely. It must legitimate the experience of disappointed needs from the past and provide an environment conducive to the expression of whatever feelings now emerge about that. This very process both heals the past wounds and provides an experience in the present of being understood and compassionately related to. But beyond that, it must help the woman distinguish between needs that can be met in the present and those that will never be met, and then decide what to do with the feelings that are stirred when needs are not met. The woman requires help in finding a way to express her sorrow, anger, despair, etc. about both current and past needs which will continue to go unmet. Even the most ordinary of disappointments take a heavy toll on a woman who has had no experience with dealing with her needs except through denial. These disappointments and what they then stir up for the woman can be worked through within the therapy relationship.

## NOTES

1. Gull, W.W., "Anorexia nervosa (apepsia hysterica, anorexia hysterica)" *Transactions of the Clinical Society*, 7:22 (London, 1874).

2. See for example Wellbourne, J., and Purgold, J., *The Eating Sickness: Anorexia, Bulimia and the Myth of Suicide by Slimming* (Brighton, 1984), who believe that the anorectic is construing the situation incorrectly and therefore needs to be guided to reconstruct her way of thinking.

3. This rather ugly formulation is used to describe the technical process that needs

to happen. Incorporation, a term used widely within psychoanalysis to connote the taking in of an idea, an object, etc. into the psyche is unsatisfactory as it literally means "to take into the body." What is required here is a noun that can express the taking up of the body into a psychosomatic unity.

4. Eichenbaum, L., and Orbach, S., *Understanding Women* (New York, 1983).

# 10   Behind the Defense

## RESTART THE DEVELOPMENT OF A SELF

The effectiveness of the work that the therapist and client engage in to understand and reverse the food refusal and to change fundamentally the woman's physical experience of self depends on restarting developmental processes that have been arrested for a considerable length of time. Anorexia is a psychological symptom and distress pattern that is the outcome of the blocking of arrested developmental processes. These developmental processes are always shaped by the particular set of cultural attitudes prevalent in contemporary Western society. The complex of forces that have resulted in a truncated development in the anorectic need to be understood in order for the attempt to restart the development to be successful. What do I mean by this?

Modern psychoanalytic theory and the contributions of feminist theories have focused attention on the infant's early relationships, on the formation of personality, and on the implications of gender in the critical "mothering" relationship. They have shifted the terrain of psychological inquiry from the Oedipus complex to the vicissitudes of object relations and to the role of the mother in the psychology of the developing person. These theories have illuminated the difficulties and ambivalences in the mother–daughter relationship that create a particular shape to women's psychology. Feminist psychoanalytic practice, meanwhile, is detailing the ways in which these difficulties and the vastly important consequences of being mother-reared can be addressed within the therapy relationship.

DIFFICULTIES WITH TAKING IN

Foremost among the observations of those with an awareness of the importance of gender in early object relations has been the discovery of the difficulties women clients in therapy experience by being on the receiving end of a relationship. The construction of femininity includes defenses against the taking in of precisely the care, contact and relating that women so desire. This observation—gleaned within both the transferential and real aspects of the therapy relationship—led to the theorizing of the essentially ambivalent nature of the mother–daughter relationship, and the understanding of how the social requirement that women must emotionally service and address the needs of others is expressed in the way in which the relating proceeds in the early mother–daughter relationship. The mother–daughter relationship is both the site of instruction and a model for future relating. In other words, the mother in psychologically fitting her daughter for her social role consciously and unconsciously inhibits her impulse to give to her on a consistent basis. At the same time, she alerts her to address those very needs in others. The care-giving and reticence to express one's own needs which are such essential features of femininity, stem then from these two sources: being schooled to give, developing the capacity to recognize and to respond to the need to be cared for in others, and not expecting that one's own needs will be met.

As we have seen, the consequences for women's psychology are that women become hesitant about the expression of their needs. The exaggeration of this is the shame that attaches to having needs in the first place. The needs exist and arise in the woman but they become trapped behind a thicket of defenses. This defense structure then serves to prevent women from both expressing and experiencing their own needs directly, and creates a structural resistance to the taking in of nurturance.

## THE VICISSITUDES OF THE DEFENSES

The developmental processes that are arrested can only be restarted if the nurturance that is required for continued emotional growth can enter the woman's truncated psyche. The fact that she has developed defenses against the taking in of precisely such nurturance poses certain therapeutic tasks. It focuses the attention of the psychotherapeutic work, in a particular direction—the contacting of the arrested or embryonic self *behind* the defense structure. To talk of relating to this truncated or undeveloped self is in no sense to imply that the therapeutic encounter aims at encouraging regression and then relating to the regressed person. Rather, the task of the therapy is to relate to the whole of what constitutes the person, the undeveloped psyche, the defense structure, the person as she or he is in the world. A relationship needs to be built up that can take account of the uneven areas of the person's psychological development so that those undeveloped areas can continue to grow and become integrated into a whole. The arrested part of the psyche is then related to within a context in which it becomes possible to harness the cognitive abilities of the more developed part of the person. This latter point is important. In anorexia it is only useful to relate to this essentially logical and cognitive self if the hidden inner self is also addressed. If not, the dialogue degenerates from a psychotherapeutic encounter to a discussion of logic. An example can perhaps best explain what is best avoided:

THERAPIST: Well, you know you need to eat more otherwise you will not gain weight [addressing the logical
part].
CLIENT: Yes, but I don't want to gain weight [defense
responds].
THERAPIST: But you say you wish to get better [addressing
the logical part].
CLIENT: I suppose so.

Contrast this with:

THERAPIST: The dilemma would seem to be that a part of
you [talking to the logical part] knows that you will
have to eat more in order to gain weight but [talking
to the inner part] you feel frightened and hesitant about
this because another part of you fears that this will
mean a loss of control.
CLIENT: I feel myself right in the middle of this conflict
. . . The struggle now, and it is an excruciating one,
is how to take the risk of eating, doing the eating that
I need to [logical and inner parts respond].

In the second of these examples, both parts, the inner and the logical, are being related to. As a result, the defense need not be activated. The client's position is accurately described, and being more fully related to she has the possibility of moving forward.

As one relates to the undeveloped self that has been

hidden behind the defense structure, several things are
happening. The possibility is open for the basic experience
of psychological malnourishment to be reversed. I say
possibility, for the therapeutic work that needs to be done
is on two fronts at once. On the one hand, the therapist
needs to relate to the undeveloped self—to be offering a
relationship that can make contact with this vulnerable
part. At the same time the therapist has to help the woman
clear the space so that she can use what is being offered.
The therapist needs to negotiate her way around the defenses that serve to shield the undeveloped self from outside contact. These defenses originally developed as a way
to protect this vulnerable self from being dismissed and
misunderstood. Once misunderstood and neglected, that
self seeing itself to be "bad" felt the necessity to protect
others from its presence. It goes into hiding. The defense
structure then works in two ways: it keeps the vulnerable,
undeveloped self hidden from those it imagines it might
harm, confuse or impose upon, while the state of being in
hiding prevents the still-needed-nurturance from getting
through.

   In the second of the examples given above the client
does not show any particular difficulty in accepting the
contact the therapist is offering. In other words, by being
understood, she is able to "take in" what is being given in
the relating. But the ability to have an exchange as useful
as the one cited depends upon the therapist's alertness to
how any particular woman's defenses work within the
therapy relationship. By this is not meant the simple interpretation of defenses such as: "You are frightened to be
close to people and contact and so you push them away.
You do that in this therapy relationship too," but rather a
compassionate stance which expresses the tension that actually exists in the person's experience of the defense. So,
for example:

THERAPIST: It seems that there is a push and pull going on here. The desire for contact and closeness gets thwarted by the equally powerful fears that emerge in you about intimacy. In this relationship we have a chance both to see how that is expressed and to find a way together through those fears.

The most effective way through the defenses is open acknowledgment and reference to them within the therapy relationship. They are accepted by both parties as aspects of the person. They are discussed both in their protective and useful senses and in their obstructionist sense. By observing and noting their appearance in the therapy relationship they can be examined, understood and reconstituted. The eradication of the obstructionist defenses becomes a shared goal of therapist and client.

Since defenses are the *sine qua non* of anorexia nervosa, dismantling them is a sensitive issue throughout the therapy. The defense structure seems to be built in layers and one needs to work through each layer. A metaphor of a house as the psyche can perhaps serve our purposes here. The plan for the house was a good one, but in the event it was built on fairly shaky foundations. Underneath the ground floor deep in the foundations of the building, both the potential strengths and structural weakness live side by side (the hidden developing self). The structural weaknesses instead of being corrected have been poured into concrete (thus the undeveloped self is frozen). In the concrete the outer walls, rather than being supported on solid beams, are jerry-rigged almost on stilts (the defenses). Their weakness needs to be constantly shored up and supports of all kinds are brought in to keep them upright. Inside the house the windows and doors fit badly. They do not provide adequate protection from the elements letting in too much heat and cold at the wrong times (the body is not felt as

safe, the environment is experienced as malevolent). The
house feels rickety and the owner has to be constantly
involved in renewal projects in order to keep it as a going
concern (the taking on of rituals to give a sense of continuity). There is no time to tend to the garden. All the energy
is spent repointing, resealing, setting ackrows, etc. (the
reworking of the body, the obsessive practices and so on).
When a surveyor (therapist) comes in to try to work with
the building dweller on the structural problems, they discover together the layers of problems that exist especially
those on the outer walls. Together they dismantle some of
the brickwork, the paintwork, the plasterboard, lining pa-
per and so on. Some of the foundation work needs to be
redone in order to continue with the basically sound original plan. They work together to restore the building to its
potential. As they identify and clear one area of outer
damage such as dry rot so they come closer to being able
to insulate the building correctly. They work patiently
through each area that needs to be redone, not expecting a
magic cure but realizing that rising damp creates wet walls
which destroys the plasterwork. The goal of the therapy is
that the therapist and the client work together carefully and
painstakingly through the defense structure, to the original
and still existing potential, so that the "building" can
achieve the glory for which it was destined.

The building process is done with grace, for above all,
the therapy and the work that the therapist and client do
together is an act of creation. It is a giving birth to an
embryonic self which, stranded on a psychic desert island,
has grown prickly, like a cactus to protect itself from the
elements. The client literally comes alive during the course
of a successful therapy. Shedding one calcified skin after
another, she feels herself to exist throughout body and
soul. She achieves a psychosomatic unity. She feels a
sense of well-being, an entitlement to what the world has

to offer; she is available for contact with others because having surmounted the psychological obstacles to "taking in" she has received the nurturance necessary for the restarting of her own developmental processes. She can now give and receive from a position of having.

This is achieved if the therapist can hold on to the focus of relating to the embryonic self behind the defenses. Defenses will arise throughout the therapy process and may be a source of confusion and despair to therapist and client alike. If the therapist is able to anticipate that change can be a difficult and painful process and that defenses will manifest themselves as ways to alert the client and the therapist to the particular difficulty of the moment, then the appearance of yet another manifestation of the defenses can be seen as not so much an expression of work not done but rather a challenge to work through that particular difficulty. Defenses can be understood during the therapy process as indicators to difficulties not sufficiently addressed. For example, after two years in therapy, Jean found it somewhat easier to express her feelings about everyday situations. Whereas she used to present either a compliant or sullen exterior she was now generally animated. When she felt sadness, grief or depression during the sessions she was able to share her feelings with the therapist (and increasingly with the outside world). Due to a sudden death in the therapist's family, the therapist extended her Easter break from two to three weeks. On the therapist's return, Jean was extremely understanding and rather nonchalant about the disruption. For the following two sessions she was quite cut off from any visible affect. She reported the events of her Easter break but seemed to be keeping back much of what she felt. The therapist understood Jean's retreat as a response to her feeling upset about the delay in the resumption of sessions. Jean, she surmised, felt let down and abandoned. She could cope

with a two-week break but the third week was very difficult for her. Part of the difficulty arose because the first
two weeks of the break had been a *positive* experience.
Jean felt good in herself and was eager to share with the
therapist the strength she found inside herself. The good
feelings quickly disappeared when she received the call
about the extension. Jean experienced the extension as
"being dropped," almost "like a punishment for the good
feelings." She became extremely anxious and appeared to
lose her newfound ways of dealing with painful feelings.
She found herself cutting back on her food and compul-
sively attending aerobics classes. She temporarily retreated
into anorectic ways of coping. She felt that she should not
show the therapist her upset, especially since the therapist
was bound to be upset herself at this time. She should not
burden her, but present an unneedy exterior. In fact she
put up such a wall that it was hard at first for the therapist
to make contact. As the therapist could help Jean recognize that she was finding it excruciatingly difficult to confront her need for her, so Jean could loosen up a bit. In this
case, then, the defense against dependency needs was
reasserting itself.

With this in mind it is not useful to judge the client for
"being defended," "acting defensive" or "using one's
defense" as intentional ways of being or the expression of
"regressing in the treatment"; rather, the appearance of a
defense at an unexpected moment is a challenge to the
therapist to help the woman work through a remaining area
of difficulty. Of course technically the defenses *are* working as a blocking mechanism, but if they are viewed solely
from such a perspective they have in effect ensnared the
therapist and the *raison d'être* of the therapeutic work—
that is, the contacting of the embryonic self—is lost.

Before I go on to say more about the value and the
effect of relating to the embryonic self, I should add that

the defenses that do occur throughout the therapy relationship can be extremely difficult to work with. If they are successful as defenses, they can induce in the therapist the intended effect—a desire to stay away and not get close. They may successfully shield the woman as though behind steel gates so that she feels impenetrable; the therapist may then have the desire to pierce the coat of armor or simply walk away put off. As the characteristically anorectic defenses of rituals, food denial and obsessions diminish, it may be the case that equally taut splitting mechanisms come into play, with the effect of keeping the therapist out. For example, when Audrey felt close to the therapist and felt especially helped and understood in a session, she was inclined to arrive exceedingly late for the following session. She would rush in excusing herself and talk speedily without feeling about "nothing much in particular." The therapist could feel a disappointment inside herself. The contact from the previous session seemed to be being undone. She found it hard to engage with Audrey's monologue and felt far from making contact. The therapist needs to keep an awareness of how the defenses do affect her or him, how they serve to discourage their efforts to keep open the contact with the developing self and at what particular points they occur in the therapy. In this way their appearance can be the signal to a speedy understanding rather than the prelude to a long and confusing patch within the therapy. The therapist suggested to Audrey that she might be in retreat from the intimacy they shared the session before. While Audrey felt helped, being helped simultaneously threatened her habitual way of doing things, that is on her own. By the therapist's addressing the difficulty in the connection it could be restarted again.

The client's defenses may be alerted whenever she has an experience of "danger." Danger as an internal warning system gets activated in a range of circumstances. A woman may sense elements of a historically painful situation being replayed in the present, when she is perched between acting as she has done in the past and trying new ways of being in the present. Danger is a subjective visceral experience rather than a logical one. Paradoxically for many women, danger is as frequently associated with doing better as it is with doing worse. Failure is something women anticipate for themselves, disappointment is an emotional state they know well, while the success or change that a woman may long for and strive for may be very hard for her simply to use and enjoy. She may "defend" against it by distrusting the change, apparently undoing her progress. For one woman, keeping her room tidy and her clothes clean was a novel experience that developed during the course of therapy. It represented a growth in self-esteem of which she was aware, but at the same time she had not yet consolidated this new self-image and from time to time she would unaccountably let the dishes in her sink stack up, leave her clothes lying around, in short create a disagreeable mess. The periods of messiness got shorter and shorter and her tidiness was not itself compulsive. It was thus as though she was testing the new her and distrusting it. Other women on the point of positive change may find themselves unspeakably anxious. They may reinstitute anorectic rituals as a way to cope. If the therapist is aware that success is problematic then she or he has a good chance of enabling the woman to push through the difficulty. By staying with her through the conflict that success stirs up, the defenses need not be so insistently activated.

It is important that the therapist remembers that the therapy relationship exists for the purpose of helping the client work through whatever difficulties occur. Thus it is the therapist's professional responsibility not to get caught up in the client's defenses. The client cannot help herself: she is in therapy for precisely that reason. The therapist needs to make a commitment to herself to be sufficiently on top of the situation to avoid getting caught in the web of the defenses; instead, she should stay giraffe-like, neck high, over, above and behind the defense, to keep the goal of contact with the hidden self clearly at the forefront. The irritation the therapist may feel, the frustration or despair that is bound to arise from time to time are part of the therapeutic relationship. This is not to advocate that the therapist discloses this in the therapy dialogue but rather that the therapist should see it as a communication from the client about how very irritated, frustrated, despairing or whatever, the woman feels about her situation. If the feeling the therapist experiences is one induced by the client, then it is probably one that the client is unable to experience directly, and so it has become split off and foisted on to the therapist. If the therapist can bear this in mind when she feels subject to these kinds of feeling in the therapy, then she will be less inclined to retreat but rather take up the phenomenon in a way useful to the client. So, for example, if the client is so listless and depressed that the therapist finds herself feeling desperately useless, then she can examine this as an expression of the client's worries about whether she will ever be able to get the help she needs. The feeling of hopelessness transmitted to the therapist introduces her emotionally to the client's experience. The therapist can make use of feelings such as these by addressing herself to the fact of the splitting mechanism, and by continuing to talk to the client behind the defense:

THERAPIST: The listlessness and despair you are experiencing can make one feel very hopeless. And I think it is useful for us to take note of the appearance of these very discouraging kinds of feeling just at a point when you were beginning to feel a bit more confidence and entitlement. It seems as though there is an ongoing conflict about having good things or experiencing yourself as all right. What we need to understand together is how the attempt to consolidate growth can get subverted by the fear of the growth so that you feel bad, hopeless, despairing inside rather than hopeful, energetic, etc.

In this example the therapist speaks to the split-off effect and to the developing self that had retreated once again behind the defenses. The client, feeling emotionally understood, is able to reappropriate feelings she was splitting off. That process allows her to "take in" within the therapy relationship and in so doing she does not find herself in retreat from the desired growth. By not acting "put off" by the defense, the therapist is able to give to the client and reverse an experience of hopelessness. By her action the therapist is indicating that she can help the client through the difficulties and that she is not destined to be stuck out in a psychic desert.

As the therapist holds on to the goal of relating to the developing self behind the defenses, she is aiding that part's development and helping the process of psychic integration. As unneeded defenses weaken and the developing self emerges more forcefully, the client begins to have an authentic experience of self and a sense of continuity between her inner and outer worlds. The attention the therapist pays to the developing self is in direct contrast to the lack of conscious attention the anorectic woman gives it. So much of the woman's efforts have been directed towards the repression of the inner self that she may feel disconcerted at first by the therapist's attempts to get in close and relate to a part of her that she has deemed so unacceptable. As she allows the therapist in, the idea that needs and vulnerabilities are wrong, bad and ugly is dissipated. The needs get directly addressed and in this way the woman develops a facility in recognizing them and responding to them. But this is to run ahead of ourselves for the moment because the relating to needs and how that occurs in the therapy relationship will be described shortly. For the present we need to turn to two other prerequisites of the therapy relationship that are evident in the examples given so far.

The first of these is how the therapy helps the client through the bad feelings that are bound to emerge during the process of recovery. (These are feelings she is habituated to splitting off and shunting into the anorectic rituals.) The second is how the therapist works alongside the client, psychically holding her hand, providing an experience of emotional reliability which can help her come to grips with the difficulties she has found herself in. In the feminist practice that has developed to address the very strong yearnings that women evince for nurturance—and the defenses against these yearnings—these two features work together. As the client is able to feel the therapist's being there for her, so she is able to risk feeling some of the pain, distress, upset and so on that has been long repressed. In other words, it is precisely the actuality and availability of a reliable emotional relationship that makes it possible for the woman to confront her inner distress. The therapist acts as the supporting external psyche that contains her, allowing her to let go sufficiently for the buried emotional wounds to emerge. By having the experience of the therapist "being in" the experience with her, her internal feelings of loneliness and isolation are mitigated. Obviously, one who is used to emotional isolation will not find its reversal a completely straightforward experience, but this of course is the very stuff of the therapy relationship—the making of intimate contact and the working through of the barriers against the intimacy.

The reader will notice that in the dialogue examples the therapist has consciously inserted her presence and the evidence of the therapist–client relationship: "together *we* can . . . or *we* have discovered . . . or as *we* have come to understand." This partnership becomes entirely explicit in the therapy. The therapist puts herself forward as an ally, and is with the client in the experience. The approach is one in which the therapist is exploring with the client rather than looking on from afar. This is not meant as invasive or cloying. There is no way in which it is helpful for the client to be "taken over" or dominated by the therapist. Rather, the efforts are directed towards providing an appropriate presence which can break through the isolation and loneliness by means of emotionally reliable interventions.

The therapist's act of inserting herself in this way into the client's experience requires sensitivity as to moment and mood. For such interventions to be neither irrelevant nor intrusive but useful, they need to be exactly on target. They need to address the woman's experience directly so that she has the feeling of being understood. These interventions become the psychological building blocks to recovery. An accurate statement by the therapist at the right moment provides a psychic hammock into which the client relaxes. Once she is supported, some of the energy that she has had to use just to keep herself going is now available for growth. Held safely, she can gradually release herself from the "stuck" position and move forward.

At the same time, this "being in tune" the therapist strives for is the attempted, but often disrupted, form of relating. The therapist works hard to "feel herself" into the client's experience, to "know" what it is the client is feeling so that the client is not alone and can sense an empathetic presence. This very being in tune may be distrusted, or the client may worry that she cannot rely on it and so may disparage the therapist's efforts or reject her comments. If this is anticipated by the therapist it need signal neither failure nor misunderstanding. It can be understood as another expression of the defense working within the therapy relationship, testing out how safe this relationship really is. For anyone who has experienced the kind of continual emotional rejection and mismatching felt by the woman, it becomes easy to understand how she has continually to test the reliability of what the therapist purports to be offering. It can help greatly to minimize the woman's agony through this "testing" if the therapist shares her understanding of the need for the testing process. It gives meaning to the action, and accurate explanations provide a way into the intimate relating that is necessary between the client and therapist.

The experience of intimate relating is difficult and exhilarating for all women in therapy, but particularly for anorectic women who have become used to a terrifyingly high level of emotional isolation. Isolation is second nature to them. There is no expectation that they can and should be accepted and understood. The anorexia has been about the very impossibility of being accepted. Being understood within the therapy relationship ushers in its own kind of pain for it makes transparent what has not happened up to that point in the woman's life. The exposure of the previous lack, and how to cope with the felt experience of it, becomes a central feature of the therapeutic work. Thus much of the content of the therapy focuses around the expression of the very pain the woman has been retreating from, and in response to which the anorexia developed originally.

This pain is hard for the woman to bear and frequently hard for the therapist too. While the woman experiences the pain as evidence of her badness, the therapist may feel acutely the pain of the client's circumstances. The woman will often wish to retreat from the pain that emerges. She is in agony and these new painful/sad/hopeless/despairing feelings seem to have a momentum of their own. She feels out of control. She fears what is psychically around the corner. Rage, vengefulness, envy, passion, competition and so on, beckon as yet more unmanageable feelings. The therapist needs to help her live in and through these dramatic feelings one by one and many, many times over so that she can reverse the experience of feeling that emotions are bad things that must be forcibly controlled.

The therapist and client live through these feelings together in various ways. The goal of this aspect of the therapeutic work is that the client be able to increase the range of emotions she can express and tolerate directly. The terror that the client associates with imagining what it would be like to experience these feelings is rarely as great as the actual experiencing of the feelings themselves. This needs to be conveyed to the woman in a gentle way. Exploring the nuances of apparently undramatic or unremarkable feelings—such as how she felt when the sun shone or when someone stopped and asked her for directions—serves the purpose of making conscious habitual and manageable feelings, thus paving the way for the expansion of her emotional vocabulary. But beyond such routine preparatory work the therapist needs to provide a consistent presence and attitude in order gently to encourage the client to express the feelings that are split-off or held in so tightly.

Audrey described her experience of this process as follows. It was as though she was poised at the edge of a cold swimming pool during a long hot summer. She needed to take the plunge but she tensed against the anticipated chill of the water. As the summer wore on, she put in a toe, then an ankle, then her lower legs. Eventually she became accustomed to the coldness of the water and found that it tempted her. She felt frustrated by her timidity. She jumped in, shivered for the first few strokes, was sure she'd made the wrong decision, but continued on until by the second length she relaxed and let the water hold her. After several minutes she was calmed and soothed. When she got out of the pool she felt lighter and refreshed. The next time she went swimming she felt the familiar hesitation. The water seemed inviting but terribly cold. She reminded herself of her last experience and took the plunge. After a length she felt that relief wash over her and she resolved to keep on swimming.

The feelings that Audrey was able to allow herself were the very same feelings she had denied and which subsequently led to the development of anorexia. The feelings that emerged were powerful and stormy, but rather than terrifying her they provided her with the most tremendous relief. Getting into the water released the energy that had gone towards tensing herself up as she dangled parts of herself in the pool. As she cried through her pain and disappointment and raged through the anger that came to the surface, she felt measurably better. She felt more "of a person." The gap between her inner and outer worlds decreased and she felt a substance and wholeness within herself—the very sureness she had been striving for with the rituals and food denial.

Although the relief Audrey felt was demonstrable, she balked during much of the process of accepting her feelings. She alternately feared facing her own feelings and exposing them to the therapist. She anticipated rejection and could not imagine anything else. Not surprisingly, it transpired that the injunction she received as a child to "wake up with a smile" meant "never show any upset or sadness." There was so much distress in the family that unthinkingly seeking an oasis from their own pain, her parents looked to her to be the happy, shining, contented

part of their lives. Thus she became extremely awkward
with dealing with emotions that weren't strictly positive,
and was convinced that they would engender rejection.
The acceptance she felt had been contingent on having a
smiling persona. She was afraid to give up the little acceptance she had. In time her fear of all of her feelings
became overwhelming. She felt terrified of acknowledging/
looking/feeling/experiencing/exposing them. The therapist
wondered what could possibly be so terrible in these feelings. In the event, the feelings were less terrifying than the
mighty defense structure that was holding them in place.

Audrey experienced an enormous relief in reconnecting
with the split-off parts of herself within the context of an
ongoing and emotionally reliable relationship. The fact
that the therapist did not reject her when she cried, when
she was desperately despairing, or when she came into
sessions in a fury, but was able to relate with her in her
distress, gave Audrey for the first time in her life the novel
experience that feelings, both pleasurable and difficult,
were and are a part of everyday life. The reappropriation
of the feelings provided a sense of solidity that all the
rituals and routines could not. Having a living, breathing,
emoting self, she could stand much more firmly on two
feet, accepting who she was without having constantly to
restructure herself physically and psychologically.

The therapist was able to be with Audrey during these
moments and show her that she was there for her by not
responding to the intent of any of the defenses. The therapist continually cleared the way for Audrey's feelings to be
expressed, at first in regard to the circumstances of her
everyday life and later as she became more comfortable
with the "having of feelings" within the therapy relationship itself. The therapist encouraged Audrey to express a
range of problematic feelings that she had towards the
therapist. Aware of the fact that such feelings were fre-

quently transferential, the therapist received the negative feelings without herself feeling attacked. She could accept whatever Audrey expressed and this acceptance mitigated some of her own worries about having and expressing negative feelings. The abreaction of such feelings alongside an understanding of where they came from, and why repression had been instituted, gave Audrey a confidence that what she was now allowing herself to feel was comprehensible and legitimate. Expressing negative feelings reduced her sense of her own fragility which up to that point kept her away from friendships, for she always felt in danger of not being able to keep her "happy" mask going. The therapist observed that the expression of these feelings changed the image that Audrey projected. She had presented herself as extremely brittle and fragile. This presentation engendered a timidity in others so that in relating to Audrey they felt themselves to be walking on egg shells. Now she began to project more confidence and solidity and although she was frequently quite angry and sad, she was also more approachable.

As the therapy relationship continued, Audrey was disappointed from time to time with the actual interventions of the therapist. This is bound to be the case in any relationship, including any therapy relationship. In the latter, acceptance of such disappointments provides the means towards a greater understanding of how very painful the mismatching of the client's need with the response of the therapist can be. Disappointments such as these are felt all the more powerfully because this may be the first relationship in which the woman experiences the possibility of being understood and indeed has felt understood. The disappointment then has to be faced squarely. The therapist needs to acknowledge that on such an occasion she may have misunderstood the client. These disappointments can be over apparently minor issues which makes them all the more difficult to track down: a chance glance at a clock during the session, the picking up on material from a dream rather than other content offered, the misunderstanding about what the particular issue might be at any one moment for the woman. These kinds of mismatchings can be experienced during the therapy as tremendous disappointments. They take on great significance. The client feels let down, dropped out of phase. She contacts her feelings of despair and hopelessness. The therapist needs to indicate that together they will be able to survive this experience, that the "mistake" is not evidence of her inability to be there, it does not mean that she is just another unsatisfactory caregiver. It is rather that sometimes she is not precisely in tune: the therapeutic encounter is about developing the facility to be in tune as much as possible and to be able to cope with the consequences of not being so should that arise.

Going through and surviving the bumps that occur in the therapeutic relationship with an anorectic is in itself very important. Incorrect interpretations or clumsiness on the part of a therapist in any therapeutic relationship is never welcome but nor is it entirely unavoidable. The therapist cannot always be absolutely on target.[1] When working with a woman who is anorectic, however, incorrect interventions can produce a situation in which the woman continues physically to come to the sessions but is in retreat behind a false self—an accommodating or withdrawn persona that hides her feelings of hurt and disappointment. Thus the therapist needs to be alert to changes she experiences in her client and to see whether they have not been stimulated by an intervention of hers that missed the point, was heavy-handed or off-base in a way that psychically "crushed" the anorectic woman. Being able to catch a "mistake" and then trace the ways in which the client has dealt with the disappointment becomes a part of their therapeutic work. In discovering the ways in which the client has tried to cope with the mistake, they are building up a sense of confidence that they will survive the difficulties that arise in their relationship. This is extremely reassuring and provides the anorectic, perhaps for the first time in her life, with a real sense that feelings of all kinds, conflicts and disappointments are part of everyday relating and intimacy. Relating is seen to involve all of one rather than just the shadowy false self that has been making such great efforts to connect with or—at the very least—to be acceptable to others up to that point.

The strong feelings that emerge during the therapy are, of course, the feelings that have been bound up in the anorexia. The denial of food has been a denial of feelings and need. As feelings previously repressed become part of the everyday experience of the woman, so needs of all kinds push themselves to the fore. This is not an exactly parallel process, but the allowing of the desire to fulfill an emotional appetite accompanies the desire to fulfill physical ones too. The restarting of the development of the self involves acquiring the skills of feeding oneself emotionally and physically. These skills can be learned in the context of a therapy relationship in which the woman comes to depend upon her therapist. Anorexia is most particularly a defense against dependency needs; it is a statement about how unneedy the woman has had to be from early on in her life. In the process of working through the anorexia she comes to accept that she does have needs and that a fundamental one is her need for a reliable emotional relationship.

The anorectic woman's sense of being a ''grown-up'' and having to take care of herself without help from another always feels precarious. As we have seen, the exercise regimens and food denial have been instituted in part as an attempt to create a boundary to keep from view the fragile inner self. They are an adolescent's attempt to create boundaries that did not arise spontaneously as a result of a smooth journey through the process of separation–individuation. Adolescence and young adulthood are the times when the person continues the process of separation from the parental base. If earlier development has proceeded relatively smoothly, young adulthood can be an exciting time in which the world outside the known—the family and the school—is stimulating and inviting. If early dependency needs were not met, as turns out to be the case with most women, then attempts at psychological separation arise from an attempt to deny the needed dependency. Inevitably the adolescent needs to construct false boundaries to achieve some sense of independence. Still needing so much, she cannot use the adolescent phase to separate from a consolidated strength, rather she has to wrench herself away and create an illusion of differentiation. She uses the rituals and food denial as a barrier between the inner hungry self and the functioning false self. In this way she can apparently separate herself from her family and the unmet needs while she simultaneously suppresses those needs.

Coming into therapy, the woman will be put in touch with the reasons for and the consequences of those attempts at separation. Inevitably she will find the notion of needs disagreeable and she will rarely discover in herself any that do not bring up in her feelings of guilt or a desire to inflict some punishment on herself. Suppressing her needs had been a way to achieve a pseudo-independence. During Jean's first year of therapy the recognition of needs and feelings was so difficult that as they occurred she would hurt herself from time to time: she would crush a glass against the wall or burn herself with a cigarette. Exposing the self-immolation she practiced was extremely painful but by our understanding together the source and the function of the guilt she was able to decrease this response. Slowly things shifted and after reporting the week's events for the first ten minutes or so of the session, she would slump back in her chair and gaze at the therapist. She began to be able to use the therapy relationship as a place just to be—an unusual experience for her and one she could barely tolerate at first. In time she came to be able to sit in this way for ten minutes and then for most of the session. It was as though the undeveloped part of her that needed just to *be* without *doing*[2] was emerging.

This state of "being" that Winnicott considers so crucial to the psychic development of self took in the nourishment it needed to help restart the thwarted developmental processes. These periods of being—feeling the therapist's presence and relying on the therapist's psyche to hold her as yet unintegrated self—were punctuated by periods of severe depressions and despair. She was initially fearful of experiencing the despair and would frantically try to get herself out of it, but gradually she was able to tolerate it and the loss contained within it. This may be a difficult time for the therapist who may feel discouraged by the woman's apparent lack of progress, but in fact Jean's capacity to feel her despair *without doing* something about it was an indicator of positive development. She was allowing herself to experience feelings she had suppressed for a very long time and she was able to have those feelings without scaring herself. By sitting and "being" in the presence of another who cared for her and could live through the pain of her despair, she was taking in what she needed. She was simultaneously able to acknowledge a need and use the therapy relationship to satisfy it.

From time to time Jean and other women in similar circumstances would notice that the obsessive thinking that had become second nature to them would re-emerge in the therapy as a kind of blocking mechanism to the expression of conflictual thoughts and desires. This was noticeable partly because it was in such contrast to the calmness of the "being" state she now experienced. The state of quiet would allow for the emergence of an uncomfortable feeling and if she were unable to give that feeling expression she would find herself caught up in either a sequence of obsessive thoughts or the need to solve a puzzle of one kind or another. It was as though her head was full of different radio shows into which she tuned automatically. Each station had a program in which she could become involved and by so doing cut herself off from the difficult feeling that prompted the obsessing in the first place. Jean found this old way of coping with difficult feelings deeply distressing but she was able to use it to realize the conflict that still existed between feeling and not feeling. With the therapist's psychic hand-holding she felt the courage to try to stay in the being, feeling state.

It was important to Jean, and to other women who were equally scared of feeling their own distress, that the therapist was able to sit with her and tolerate her despair. The therapist was not required to do anything special about the feelings. She needed to acknowledge them and respect the space they required in the woman's life and in the therapy relationship. *Painful feelings require tolerance and living with and through rather than action.* At first the inactivity will be excruciating to the woman who has become highly skilled at distancing herself from feeling in various ways. She will want to know what to do with such feelings. As the therapist indicates a relaxed approach and receives the feelings in the therapy relationship, so the woman becomes more accustomed to expressing them. The fact that the therapist could convey an assurance that painful times could be tolerated gave Jean the confidence to believe that she too could live through them. They would destroy neither her nor the therapist.

The anorectic woman tends to believe that the negative and alarming feelings that live inside her are as frightening to the therapist as they are to her and obviously were to those closely involved in her upbringing. This kind of fear of negative feelings stems from their inability to be tolerated in the family. In woman after woman who has had anorexia, a message that has entered them forcefully from the culture at large, and within the family, was that they should project a sense of being all right. The insistence that women should always be available to provide nurturance to others may preclude recognition and expression of their own negative feelings. This does not mean that they were able to do this, for certainly many women who come to have anorexia were openly rebellious as youngsters and teenagers. For women whose anorexia developed as a way to bring order to a chaotic homelife, the rebellion was accompanied by enormous guilt and a hidden desire to respond to the parental message that they should project contentment.

Whatever the actual circumstances of the woman's growing up, one thing is clear—that the parental figures were unable to absorb and contain the normal range of distress children express. Thus the anorectic has an inordinate fear of negative feelings. She experiences them as calamitous, and a constant theme during the therapy process will be a question about whether it is really all right to "impose" these upset feelings on the therapist or to bring them in to the therapist. There is a fear that the therapist will withdraw and that the exposure of upset will produce the same kind of response it did in parental figures. Alerted to this dynamic, the therapist can talk to this worry on the part of the woman, not just once during the course of the therapy, but several times, so that gradually the refrain enters the woman's experience and she can begin to change a deeply held pattern of relating.

Not everyone is able to use the therapy situation as did
Jean. I have worked with women who were not able to
contain the chaos that had been lurking inside during the
session time who felt and acted frantic. Some women who
had only occasionally binged before they started therapy
found that as they loosened their grip on their tightly
held-in feelings, they felt panicked and wanted to eat
everything in sight to stuff them down again. The hard-
won control on which so much of their—albeit fraudulent—
self-esteem rested broke, and the opposite of the control
was unleashed in eating binges, violent episodes, fits of
spontaneous crying and so on. The woman in therapy may
feel extremely discouraged by such events and the therapist may feel inclined towards discouragement too. I would
suggest, however, that such occurrences represent an important developmental phase within the therapy. All that
has been held back is coming to the fore and the content of
the chaos can be examined. The woman now has someone
on her side with whom she can go through it. She is not
alone with the terror and uncontrollability of the chaos, so
she does not have to keep pre-empting its expression. It
can come up, be experienced and act as a purgative. The
fear of the chaos gradually dissipates as its content is
shared in the therapy relationship. An intimate enabling
relationship makes possible the experiencing and containing of feelings that the woman has feared "made her
crazy."

The capacity to feel in the context of a supportive
relationship is the key feature in the restarting of arrested
developmental processes. The therapist provides a psychological umbilical cord[3] from which the woman can both
feed herself and be fed. The corrective emotional food
then makes it possible for her to approach the wider environment differently as a potential source of self-expression
and nurture. In allowing herself to feel and to act she

reverses some of the key features of socialization towards femininity. She has been brought up to enable others to potentiate by encouraging them explicitly and by taking care of their emotional lives. In becoming anorectic she has demonstrated her profound discomfort with that role. She has refused the confines of femininity. She has demanded the right to control her body and her life and has insisted on a cause of her own. In working through the anorexia that cause becomes explicit and legitimate. She becomes a person with legitimate desires and demands which she can now openly express.

## NOTES

1. Indeed if she or he is perfect, they run the risk of being "too good a mother." Winnicott points out (Winnicott, D.W., *The Maturational Process and the Facilitating Environment* (London, 1965)) that problems can arise when experienced mothers are so skilled at reading their children's messages that they anticipate everything and thus unwittingly deny their children the experience of disappointment or mastery.
2. Winnicott, *ibid.*
3. Eichenbaum, L. and Orbach, S., *Understanding Women* (New York, 1983).

# 11   Medical Issues

When a therapist first meets an anorectic woman, she cannot help but be aware of several striking physical features. Firstly there is the physical diminution, which may be accompanied by a puffy face and prominent eyes. Unless it is the height of summer, the woman will doubtless be wearing many layers of clothing, to keep her warm and to disguise her level of thinness. If she is not well clad her body will have a skeletal-type appearance and her skin may well be blotchy. If asked about any physical symptoms, she may mention that her extremities are uncomfortably cold, her stomach feels distended whenever she eats, she is constipated, suffers from insomnia and an excess of energy. Many of the symptoms that arise from chronic starvation are not immediately obvious, however, either to the observer or to the sufferer.

Because serious physical problems are associated with starvation—all of which can be reversed as the woman comes to eat regularly above a certain threshold—many therapists are disinclined to take on an anorectic for fear that they do not understand the medical side of things. This can mean that a therapist, who would not hesitate to take on someone with very obvious mental symptoms of a fairly extreme nature, would be reluctant to work with an anorectic for fear of seeing her wasting away, of not being able to help the person reverse the pattern of starvation, or of encountering a medically qualified person who is in a position to come along and be critical of a treatment protocol that does not include refeeding.

Working with anorectics has become imbued with a certain aura. Because the hallmarks of anorexia are so neatly definable—much more so than is the case in general in a therapist's case-load—anorectics come to be classified or thought of in a particular way. They have a certain mystique which either interests or especially worries therapists. It may make the therapist cautious in all sorts of ways and it may lead her or him to feel more vulnerable when working with an extremely low-weight anorectic than would be the case with a similarly troubled client, for example a woman with debilitating phobias and obsessions.

This chapter has two main aims. Firstly there is the wish to provide the psychotherapist with an overview of the medical implications that arise from anorexia. A second function is to address physicians working with anorectics. I have not chosen to discuss the various biomedical theories of the etiology of anorexia nervosa which some medically-oriented researchers have advanced, as the overwhelming evidence lies in the direction of social and psychological explanations. A medical training may lead one to think in terms of a medical hypothesis but in the case of anorexia it is especially unconvincing. A biomedical theory cannot successfully account for the rise in anorexia, the incidence of episodic bulimia and the Western cultural obsession with thinness.

To turn now to the primary function of this chapter: therapists need to know how to evaluate the situation of a particular client and to understand the possible medical danger she is in. Briefed in this way, the therapist can make realistic interventions without a nagging fear that the intervention is inappropriate. Beyond this the therapist may feel less awed by the recital of an array of dire physical symptoms apparently requiring immediate hospitalization, and an inclusive treatment package from the medical establishment. It can be daunting to cooperate with medical personnel if one feels ignorant of medical terminology relating to diagnosis and treatment.[1] It can be even more difficult to propose changes in a medically instituted treatment protocol if one feels oneself to be ignorant of the medical picture. In addition one may find it hard to question what are finally matters of *judgment* rather than *fact* if the symptomatology of the anorectic remains described firmly within medical nomenclature. As non-medical practitioners become versed in medical nomenclature they may then find that they are less intimidated by engaging with medics.

A list of the most usual symptoms and implications follows with their technical and pedestrian vocabulary. Two literature reviews, one by Sours[2] (with an accompanying medical glossary) and one by Garfinkel and Garner[3] go some way to helping the non-medical practitioner to understand the physical implications of anorexia nervosa. Palmer's[4] extensive discussion of the hormonal (the neuroendocrinal) aspects of anorexia provides a useful summary of current hypotheses about changes that anorexia effects in central nervous system functioning. A possible drawback to these reviews from the point of view of the non-medical practitioner is that they may convey the impression that all women who come to suffer from anorexia manifest the extreme symptomatology they discuss. With this caveat understood, I do recommend that non-medical practitioners familiarize themselves with the current medical thinking.

Starvation causes numerous changes in normal body functioning. Almost every organ, the blood (hematological system), and the skin (epidermis) respond to severe undernourishment by, in essence, slowing down. In themselves these symptoms are not necessarily dire but are rather indicators that the body is underfunctioning in some way. Thus skeletal development may be stunted during the period of malnutrition; low blood pressure (hypotension) is reasonably common; the heartbeat slows (bradycardia); circulatory disturbances (such as Raynaud's phenomenon) mean that extremities are vulnerable to cold; neurological changes are reflected in electroencephalograph (EEG) readings; the immunological functions become impaired so that the body becomes both increasingly vulnerable to infection and less able to fight it off; an irregular heartbeat (arrythmia) can occur during exercise and so on. The clinical picture of the abstaining anorectic is thus not a cheering one. It is as though the body's motor has gone into hibernation and is fulfilling its basic "mechanical" functions on one cylinder fed with cheap-quality petrol. The real dangers that flow from severe undernourishment are that the motor will finally not be able to go on, and that cardiac arrest will occur.

While starvation implies a slowing down of body functioning in general and an inability for tissue repair to occur as a matter of course, the effects of binging and vomiting or excessive use of laxatives compound the medical picture in particularly worrying ways. The teeth, for example, can become especially vulnerable to the effects of reverse saliva from vomiting which causes tooth decay, loss of enamel and gum disease. A bloated skin (oedema) is also characteristic in binging anorectics. The overriding problem and the fear in practitioners' minds (both medical and non-medical) is of cardiac arrest due to electrolyte imbalance.

Potassium is an iron which circulates in the bloodstream

so the nerves can function. Hypokalemia, which is a lowering of the level of potassium in the blood, leads to a wide range of complications, the most severe of which are muscle weakness, paralysis, occasional neurological disturbances such as *grand mal* fits and kidney (renal) function problems, and cardiac arrest which can come out of the blue. Hypokalemia is particularly insidious because the heavy laxative use and vomiting which void the body of potassium can be gradual and unremarkable from the outside, causing serious complications without observable physical changes. It is this inability to detect what is going on that is most worrying, and renders therapists fearful of working with anorectic women. As hypokalemia is associated with binging and vomiting or laxative use and weight loss, practitioners would be wise to search out a sympathetic physician with whom to cooperate so that out-patient treatment benefits from regular monitoring of potassium levels.

I have stated elsewhere that a minimum condition for working with an anorectic on an out-patient basis must be that she agrees not to go below the weight at which she enters the treatment situation. A stable low weight, I argued, need not in itself spell medical danger and in fact in the case of non-binging anorectics, electrolyte imbalance does not in itself pose the same kind of hazard that exists for the bulimic anorectic.

To turn now to the second function of this chapter: medically qualified people who do not specialize in the treatment of anorexia can feel tremendously at sea, when they do come across individual cases in the course of their work. Refeeding techniques are diligently tried and while the patient may appear to get better the weight gain is frequently not sustained. The medical practitioner quite understandably feels frustrated and may seek a more complete refeeding package with closer supervision, more em-

phasis on behavior modification and so on. Because medics
are trained to see the body in its component parts (although
a more holistic approach is now being taken up) and to
thus treat the anorectic patient as being symptomatic and
hence in need of treatment at a physiological level, a
medical perspective may offer false hope or orientate treatment in unpromising ways.[5] Imbalances in brain bio-
chemistry have led some researchers[6] to administer psycho-
tropic drugs in the hope that these will produce relief from
binging patterns. While undoubtedly some patients will
benefit from intervention at a bio-chemical level, for many
others they are not simply a false hope but reduce the
complex of psycho-social problems bound up in the distressing symptoms—the meaning of the anorexia—to a bio-
chemical puzzle. Looked at this way, treatment has little
chance of addressing the profound psychological issues
involved in the taking-up of anorexia.

Just as the non-medical practitioner has need of the
physician, so the physician needs the skills or cooperation
of psychologically trained personnel in the treatment of
anorexia. The approach as outlined in the second half of
this book is an attempt to lay the groundwork for what a
psychological intervention should look like. In other words,
physicians may be able to adapt the proposed guidelines to
the parameters of their treatment situation and in so doing
be more effective than if they rely on bio-chemical or
simple behavioral approaches.

It is likely that during the course of time one will come
across an anorectic whose medical condition is such that it
would be hazardous for her to be without intensive treatment and medical monitoring. Or it may be that a particularly low weight anorectic may herself wish to be in a
contained environment which will help her over the first
hurdles of learning how to eat again. If one turns to the
conventional hospital programs one invariably comes

across a treatment mode that is questionable on legal and ethical grounds.

In Great Britain, the Mental Health Act of 1983 provides for the compulsory admission to psychiatric hospitals of persons who are considered to be at grave risks to themselves. Under Section III of the Act, the individual can be committed for a period of up to six months. While "sectioning" anorectics is a contentious issue,[7] committing anorectics is a reasonably common occurrence and raises uncomfortable legal and moral questions. For the "treatment" proffered in many in-patient units is coercive, infantilizing and punitive. The patient is confined to a cubicle, forced to use a commode, sedated and cajoled to eat amounts well beyond the size of normal meals in order to gain weight speedily. Personal liberty is further restricted in the form of how often the patient may bathe, who may visit, a taboo on the bringing in of special foods, and restrictions on the involvement of out-patient psychiatric services or support services such as self-help groups. While the cases that actually require hospitalization form only a small proportion of those who suffer with anorexia it is nevertheless worth sketching out what a hospital or in-patient treatment facility that took into account the theory as advanced in this book might look like. It is not my purpose to discuss in any detail what a treatment program would look like. Rather, I wish to indicate the basis from which one might begin to think of designing one.

If we take as important the anorectic's fear of showing her dependency needs and at the same time her need to "let go" and "be looked after," then one would want to consider setting up a situation in which this conflict could be respected and addressed. In other words, both her resilience and her desire to give up all control to another needs to be taken into account rather than the former being battled with and the latter being taken advantage of. This inner conflict would form part of the therapeutic dialogue with the patient. Her inner dilemma would be discussed with her and the various implications that the period of residential treatment has for her. The residential facility itself may be experienced as a containing caregiver in which the women can begin to let down her guard without fear that she will be rendered passive. Her shame at her wish to be looked after could be addressed and sympathetic explanations offered for the way in which her dependency needs jostle inside with their very opposite. Her role in the treatment plan would be as a genuine partner. The difficulties likely to be encountered would be discussed on a regular basis so that ways of working with them could be envisioned. We can see how a genuinely sympathetic treatment situation in which the woman has the chance to be with other women who are struggling with the same difficulties could help enormously. The isolation and the desperation that flow from anorexia are fractured, and the protected environment provides the context for working through the difficulties, with taking in food; being able to keep it inside; coping with changes in body size and the anticipation and onset of menstruation, etc. The very difficult issues that are stirred as the individual begins to eat again could be discussed and worked through in a benevolent environment.

In most conventional treatment programs the doctors, psychiatric nurses, social workers and psychotherapists on the ward are thrust into an impossible dual role by the very design of a treatment program that has the caregiver simultaneously in the role of the enforcer of feeding, and the supposed provider of a therapeutic situation. The stress on eating is frequently accompanied by coercive measures such as guarding the patient while, or until, she ingests her food, and the taking away of "privileges" until eating is

regularized and a certain weight achieved. Food preferences of the anorectic are not respected, indeed in some
treatment programs the patient's fear of food is dealt
with by "feeding" her up with calorie-rich drinks, bypass-
ing solid food altogether. An opportunity for the person to
learn how to eat again is smothered under a threatening
insistence that she must eat. The "therapeutic" effectiveness of the caregivers is seriously eroded as they become
identified with the heavy hand of authority. The rationale
for such treatment procedures is that the patient has "shown
herself to be immature and incapable of being responsible." She has "regressed to a pre-adolescent, i.e. a childlike state in which decisions must be made for her." Her
logic is faulty and her thinking is at any rate impaired by
the effects of starvation. Such a stance on the part of
sections of the medical establishment leads frequently to
tortuous battles in which the belligerent "child" is the
recipient of a passification program "in her best interests." While not wishing to underestimate the frustration
and worry that all practitioners who work with anorectics
feel, this very "belligerence" is stoked up by the attitude
taken towards the anorectic in the first place.

It seems to me that therapeutic effectiveness is the most
important part of what a protected environment needs to
provide. The anorectic genuinely requires help and needs
to be understood, not tricked, manipulated, cajoled or
infantilized. She needs to be treated as someone who has for
complex reasons placed herself in grave medical circumstances that require immediate attention. The fact that she
finds eating so very difficult and the idea of gaining weight
so impossible and horrible needs to be accepted by the
therapeutic staff. This means that they do not argue with
her, or try to make her see sense, or tell her they know
best, or undervalue her feelings, but enter into a relationship with her in which the stated purpose is to understand

the medical and psychological dilemma the woman is in so that together they can help her through a very difficult period. At a dangerously low weight there will need to be some agreed-upon minimum to be eaten daily. However, I remain unconvinced that such an agreement would necessarily have to be coercive. Respect for the patient coupled with a discussion of the seriousness of the situation can yield extremely good results on an out-patient basis. One should be able to translate this into a residential setting. One would wish to avoid at all costs the following dialogue around food which all too often goes like this:

PSYCHIATRIC NURSE: Eat it up, you know you must gain weight. You know you are very weak.

PATIENT: I don't want to eat. I'd rather die.

PSYCHIATRIC NURSE: Don't be silly.

PATIENT: I shan't eat it. I won't die.

PSYCHIATRIC NURSE: Look I'm afraid you will just have to eat it. I am going to sit here until it is all gone. You might as well get it over sooner than later. Anyway it tastes better hot than cold.

PATIENT: I shan't eat it. You won't make me. I hate this place.

A stand-off follows. Eventually the dialogue is repeated; perhaps the patient throws the food on the floor. Perhaps she is made to eat another plate or the same plate. She searches frantically to find a place to deposit the ingested food. The window is locked, her side-table has no drawers and she is not allowed to leave the cubicle to go to the toilet. She jumps out of her bed and exercises frantically. After a few minutes a nurse pulls the curtains and scolds her for being out of bed, brings some sedative and continues to assert her authority in questionable ways.

In the kind of environment that I am proposing such a

situation simply could not arise. Eating would be part of a process that involved preparing food, talking about how one was feeling doing so, anticipating eating and all the difficulties which that aroused, eating in the most congenial environment possible for the individual, i.e. either alone or with another person or possibly in a small group, eating small portions and seeing how the food felt in the stomach as well as how it felt psychologically. A therapeutic dialogue would be inclined to run as follows.

PSYCHIATRIC NURSE: Well, this bowl of salad that you've prepared looks very beautiful, how does it feel to you to imagine eating it?

PATIENT: It doesn't get much easier, I still dread it even though I have been able to get it down several times.

PSYCHIATRIC NURSE: Does it help to remind yourself that you have had previous helpings and nothing terrible *has* happened?

PATIENT: Well, that is what I have to do because I tend to focus on how it is going to make me bloated and fat and so on.

PSYCHIATRIC NURSE: I do appreciate how very difficult this continual struggle you have to make is and yet it is essential. Continuing to eat and not getting bloated or "fat" is reinforcing the idea that food isn't so terrible.

PATIENT: And of course I hate to admit it, but I am feeling a bit better in some ways, less speedy. Sometimes, though, when I have the salad I discover just how starving I am and that is when I panic, thinking I'll just raid everything in the hospital kitchen.

PSYCHIATRIC NURSE: Yes, and it is well of you to remind us of that fear. But we can handle that as we did last time. If as you are nearing the end of the salad you feel desperate, then we can talk about what else you might like and we can have you imagine eating it and seeing how that feels in your body before you lunge right into it. Who knows, you might even feel you could have something else and that you would enjoy it without it turning into a binge.

In this dialogue the difficulty is addressed straightforwardly with both the psychiatric nurse and the patient working on the side of the aspect of the anorectic who is trying to eat. Motivation to eat or get better is not in itself a sufficient condition for recovery. The process of coming to terms with food as a pleasurable and non-terrifying part of life, the development of secondary sexual characteristics, the putting on of weight and living in a larger body, are, as we have seen, extremely difficult for the anorectic. They require support and understanding along the way. As the above example illustrates, the nurse's anticipation of the patient's difficulty (as opposed to the disparaging of it) makes it possible for a genuine dialogue to occur which in itself provides a safety net of containment.

Obviously a program of the kind I am suggesting requires a rethinking of the treatment of in-patient anorectics and the challenging of attitudes towards them. The involvement of recovered anorectics would be most essential in the design of the program, for so many ex-anorectics have painfully and bitterly expressed what was wrong with the treatment they have received and some have begun to think about what kind of positive steps could usefully be incorporated into a treatment program. The staff of such a program would need to have very clear feelings about their own attitudes towards food, slimness and the objectification of women's bodies, so that the patient's issues were free from being muddled in with their own. It should be said that some of the struggles that occur on in-patient units currently are exacerbated by the practitioner's envy (perhaps unconscious) and irritation at the anorectics' easy ability to resist food. Many psychiatric nurses, psychotherapists, physiotherapists, social workers, dieticians and doctors (like the rest of the population) suffer from a form of compulsive eating and feel the need to be denying or depriving themselves of food in one way or another. The anorectic's persistent refusal plays into their own difficulties around control, thus adding energy to the already instituted power struggle. Thus a residential treatment program must start from the practitioners' examination of their own attitudes towards food, fat, thinness and femininity just as I have suggested such issues require clarification for psychotherapists in general working with anorectics.

The general parameters, then, of a residential treatment program for anorectics would require first, the recognition on the staff's part that anorectics have rights like all human beings and that their "illness" does not render them incompetent. The stringent control on dependency needs characteristic of anorexia needs to be recognized, as does its opposite, the wish to be cared for. The force of the food denial is to be worked with, which means it needs to be understood in its actuality and its symbolic meanings. The establishment of a therapeutic milieu is of paramount importance where the goal of the staff is to engage with the whole person, not simply the anorexia. The unit would be involved in its own food preparation, which means that it would need to be extremely flexible.

## NOTES

1. Dr. Irene Patterson points out that passage through medical school increases the student's vocabulary by 50 percent!
2. Sours, John A., *Starving to Death in a Sea of Objects: The Anorexia Nervosa Syndrome* (Aronson, New York, 1980).

3. Garfinkel, P. and Garner, D., *Anorexia Nervosa: A Multi-Dimensional Perspective* (Brunner and Mazel, New York, 1982).

4. Palmer, R.L., *Anorexia Nervosa* (Penguin, London, 1980).

5. Geoffrey Cannon reported in the *Observer* on 7 September 1984, the contents of a letter to *The Lancet* from Dr. D. Latto in which he discussed the relationship between zinc deficiencies and loss of appetite. If it encourages false hope, this article is evidence of irresponsible behavior.

6. Pope, G.H. and Hudson, J.I., *New Hope for Binge Eaters* (Harper and Row, New York, 1984).

7. "Doctor's Dilemma," BBC TV, 29 January 1985.

I would like to thank Dr. Robin Vicary for checking the medical data as cited in this chapter.

# Afterword

The tragic phenomenon of women systematically depriving themselves of food is only one example of a wide range of behaviors which women routinely exhibit. The vicissitudes of socially constructed notions of the female form make it extremely difficult for the individual woman to feel secure and at ease, whatever the size and shape of her body. While the pursuit of thinness in anorexia stands as a graphic metaphor for our time, women's eating problems of all kinds arise out of the individual's attempt both to conform to and repudiate the current aesthetic idealization of women.

A woman's idea of herself in her body inevitably reflects her internalization of prevailing social attitudes. A contributing factor or detractor in her self-esteem stems from her assessment of how in or out of step she is with contemporary standards of female attractiveness. We can understand this clearly if we imagine the following circumstances. The aesthetic standards suddenly swing in the opposite direction and the Rubenesque woman becomes *the* motif of the time. Everywhere—in magazines, television, movies, advertisements, shop mannequins—women of ample proportion now represent all that is good, beauti-

246

ful, sensual, sexual, vital, youthful, energetic and healthy. Fashion is shown on large women, health articles extol the virtues of having a good appetite and offer advice on how those who are skinny can increase their food intake. Accompanying photos, line drawings and glossy presentations of glamorous, large/fat women reinforce this new ideal. Now it is fatness that assumes a moral principle and becomes a highly regarded value. Women who are small-framed suffer the indignity of feeling skinny, they try to disguise their thin bodies by skill in dressing, perhaps by wearing false bras and bustles: they may engage in body-building programs and ingest calorie-rich products which claim to put on weight.

All manner of psychological issues are folded into the desire to be fat. Fatness is now an expression of self-esteem and self-love. Thinness is seen as a retreat from the feminine and the sexual. To be thin is to be disregarded, judged at a distance, to be seen as lacking. Thin women are in despair. Whatever they do their bodies seem to defeat them. They cannot maintain a weight gain. They feel they have failed at an essential level of femininity.

As long as aesthetic standards as preposterous and capricious as those with which we live continue to apply, and as long as such aesthetics are manipulated in the pursuit of profit on the one hand and control on the other, women will have the most enormous difficulty in finding a lasting personal solution to body-image problems. As long as bodies are by proxy the standard for women's self-evaluation and the evaluation of others, women will have difficulty with their food and with their body-image. As we extend the scope of women's lives and avenues of self-expression and transform the social arrangements that have produced our current circumstances, we can anticipate a change in the way that daughters are raised and valued in our society.

# Bibliography

Banner L., *American Beauty* (New York, 1983).

Beck, S., Bertholle, L. and Child, J., *Mastering the Art of French Cooking* (New York, 1961).

Belotti, E.G., *Little Girls* (New York, 1977).

Binswanger, L., "The case of Ellen West." In R. May *et al.* (eds.), *Existence* (New York, 1958).

Boskind-White, M. and White, W.C., *Bulimarexia: The Binge/Purge Cycle* (New York, 1983).

Braverman, H., *Labor and Monopoly Capital* (New York, 1978).

Brownmiller, S., *Femininity* (London, 1984).

Bruch, H., *Eating Disorders; Obesity, Anorexia Nervosa, and the Person Within* (New York, 1973).
   *The Golden Cage: The Enigma of Anorexia Nervosa* (New York, 1978).

Chesler, P., *Women and Madness* (New York, 1972).

Chodorow, N., *The Reproduction of Mothering. Psychoanalysis and the Sociology of Gender* (Berkeley, 1978).

Coward, R., *Female Desire* (London, 1984).

Crisp, A.H., *Anorexia Nervosa: Let Me Be* (London, 1980).

Crisp, A.H., Palmer, R.L. and Kalucy, R.S., "How Common is Anorexia Nervosa? A prevalence study," *British Journal of Psychiatry,* 128 (1976), 549–54.

Dally, P.J. and Gomez, J., *Anorexia Nervosa* (London, 1979).

*Obesity and Anorexia Nervosa: A Question of Shape* (London, 1980).

Dinnerstein, D., *The Mermaid and The Minotaur: Sexual Arrangements and Human Malaise* (New York, 1976).

Duddle, M., "An Increase of Anorexia Nervosa in a University Population," *British Journal of Psychiatry,* 123, 711–12.

Ehrenreich, B. and English, D., *For Her Own Good: 150 years of the experts of advice to women* (London, 1979).

Eichenbaum, L. and Orbach, S., *Understanding Women: A Feminist Psychoanalytic Approach* (New York, 1983).

*What Do Women Want?* (London, 1983).

Ewan, E. and Ewan, S., *Channels of Desire* (New York, 1982).

Fairbairn, W.R.D., *Psychoanalytic Studies of the Personality* (London, 1952).

Fairbairn, C.G., *Binge-eating and Bulimia Nervosa* (London, 1982).

Flax, J., "The conflict between nurturance and autonomy in mother–daughter relationships and within feminism," *Feminist Studies 4* (2) (Maryland, June 1978).

Fransella, F. and Crisp, A.H., "Comparisons of Weight Concepts in Groups of Neurotic, Normal and Anorexic Females," *British Journal of Psychiatry,* 134, 79–81.

Freud, A., "The Psychoanalytic Study of Infantile Feeding Disturbances," *Psychoanalytic Study of the Child,* 2, 119–32.

Friedan, B., *The Feminine Mystique* (New York, 1963).

Friend, A. and Metcalf, A., *Slump City* (London, 1981).

Garfinkel, P.E. and Garner, D., *Anorexia Nervosa: A Multi-Dimensional Perspective* (New York, 1982).

Garner, D. and Garfinkel, P.E., *Handbook of Psychotherapy for Anorexia Nervosa and Bulimia* (New York, 1984).

Garson, B., *All The Live-Long Day* (New York, 1975).

Goodsitt, A., "Anorexia Nervosa," *British Journal of Medical Psychology*, 42, 109–18.

Gull, W.W., *Apepsia hysterica: Anorexia Nervosa.* Transcripts of the Clinical Society of London, 7, 22–8.

Guntrip, H., *Schizoid Phenomena and Object Relations Theory* (New York, 1969).

Hirschmann, J. and Zaphitopoulos, L., *Are You Hungry?* (New York, 1985).

Hite, S., *The Hite Report* (New York, 1976).

Hurst, A.F., Lacey, L.H. and Crisp, A.H., "Teeth, Vomiting and Diet; a Study of Dental Characteristics of 17 Anorexia Nervosa Patients," *Postgraduate Medical Journal*, 53, 298–305.

Kalucy, R.S., Crisp, A.H. and Harding, B., "A Study of 56 Families with Anorexia Nervosa," *British Journal of Medical Psychology*, 50, 381–95.

Keys, A., Brozek, J., Henschel, A., Micklesen, O. and Taylor, H.L., *The Biology of Human Starvation* (Minneapolis, 1950).

Khan, M.Masud R., *The Privacy of The Self* (London, 1974).

Kinsey, A.C., Pomeroy, W.B., Martin, C.E. and Gebhard, P.H., *Sexual Behavior in the Human Female* (Philadelphia, 1949).

Koedt, A., *The Myth of the Vaginal Orgasm* (New York, 1970).

Lacey, J.M., "Sexuality and Body Weight in Normal,

Anorectic and Obese Young People,'' *Journal of the Institute of Health Education*, 16 (1978), 73–5.

Lambley, P., *How to Survive Anorexia* (London, 1983).

Lawrence, M., *The Anorexic Experience* (London, 1984).

Levenkron, S., *The Best Little Girl in the World* (New York, 1978).

   *Treating and Overcoming Anorexia Nervosa* (New York, 1983).

Macleod, S., *The Art of Starvation* (London, 1981).

Mahler, M., Pine, F. and Bergman, A., *The Psychological Birth of the Human Infant* (New York, 1975).

Marcuse, H., *Eros and Civilization* (Boston, 1955).

Masters, W.H. and Johnson, V.E., *Human Sexual Response* (Boston, 1966).

Mintz, I.L., *et al.*, *Fear of Fat* (New York, 1983).

Minuchin, S., Rosman, B.L. and Baker, L., *Psychosomatic Families: Anorexia Nervosa in Context* (Cambridge, Mass., 1978).

Mitchell, J., *Women's Estate* (New York, 1973).

Money, J. and Erhardt, A., *Man and Woman, Boy and Girl: The Differentiation and Dimorphism of Gender Identity from Conception to Maturity* (Baltimore, 1973).

Moynihan, D., *The Negro Family: The Case for National Action* (Washington DC, 1965).

Orbach, S., *Fat is a Feminist Issue* (London, 1978).

   *Fat is a Feminist Issue II* (London, 1982).

Palazzoli, M.Selvini, *Self-Starvation. From the Intrapsychic to the Transpersonal Approach to Anorexia Nervosa* (London, 1974).

Palmer, R.L., *Anorexia Nervosa* (London, 1980).

Pope, G.H. and Hudson, J.I., *New Hope For Binge Eaters* (New York, 1984).

Russell, G.F.M. ''Bulimia Nervosa: An Ominous Variant of Anorexia Nervosa,'' *Psychological Medicine*, 9 (1979), 429–48.

Schwartz, D., Thompson, M. and Johnson, C., "Anorexia Nervosa and Bulimia: The Socio-cultural Context," *International Journal of Eating Disorders*, 1, 20–36.

Sherfey, M.J., *The Nature and Evolution of Female Sexuality* (New York, 1972).

Sorlie, P., Gordon, T. and Kannel, W., "Body Build and Mortality, the Framingham Study," *Journal of the American Medical Association*, 243 (1980), 1828–31.

Sours, John A., *Starving to Death in a Sea of Objects: The Anorexia Nervosa Syndrome* (New York, 1980).

Spitz, R., *The First Year of Life: A Psychoanalytic Study of Normal and Deviant Development of Object Relations* (New York, 1965).

Turkel, S., *Working* (New York, 1974).

Vincent, L.M., *Competing with the Sylph* (New York, 1979).

Wellbourne, J. and Purgold, J., *The Eating Sickness. Anorexia, Bulimia and the Myth of Suicide by Slimming* (Brighton, 1984).

Winnicott, D.W., *The Maturational Processes and the Facilitating Environment* (London, 1965).

*Primary Maternal Preoccupation; Collected Papers* (London, 1958).

Wooley, O.W. and Wooley, S.C., "The Beverley Hills Eating Disorder: the Mass Marketing of anorexia nervosa," *International Journal of Eating Disorders*, 1, 57–69.

# Index